Prentice Hall

ChemGuide

Essentials of Chemistry

PRENTICE HALL
Upper Saddle River, New Jersey
Needham, Massachusetts

ISBN 0-13-436234-9

1 2 3 4 5 6 7 8 9 10   02 01 00 99 98

PRENTICE HALL

JUL 0 4 2002

Contents

Welcome to the ChemGuide: Essentials of Chemistry

ChemGuide: Essentials of Chemistry is an outline that summarizes ten essentials, or big ideas, in chemistry, and guides you through your studies. After reading each lesson, you can review what you learned, test your vocabulary skills, and find out what you have learned.

Introduction to ChemGuide: Essentials of Chemistry

The Introduction to the *ChemGuide: Essentials of Chemistry* explains what the essentials are and how they can help you learn chemistry.

Description of the ChemGuide: Essentials of Chemistry

Each of the ten essentials on pages 5–102 consists of four parts. The first part introduces and explains the key concepts of the essential. The second part summarizes the key concepts and outlines the topics covered in the essential. The third part helps you review the key vocabulary terms introduced in the essential. The last part gives you a chance to test yourself and find out what you have learned.

Math Refresher

You will need to have certain math skills to solve problems in chemistry. The Math Refresher helps you review those skills and practice applying them to chemistry problems.

Final Assessment

The Final Assessment is designed to give you practice taking an end-of-course examination in chemistry. It includes questions about concepts you have learned in the ten essentials.

Glossary

The Glossary contains the definitions of the boldface key terms that are presented and explained in the essentials.

Introduction to ChemGuide: Essentials of Chemistry

What are the Essentials?

- *ChemGuide: Essentials of Chemistry* was designed to provide you with an outline, or review, of the essential ideas of chemistry.

- The ten essential ideas that are covered in the *ChemGuide: Essentials of Chemistry* are as follows:

1. Energy and Matter
2. Atomic Structure and Bonding
3. Chemical Reactions
4. States of Matter
5. Chemical Equilibrium
6. Acids and Bases
7. Redox Chemistry
8. Kinetics and Thermodynamics
9. Nuclear Chemistry
10. Organic Chemistry

Description of the ChemGuide: Essentials of Chemistry

Introduction and Key Concepts

- Each essential has a lesson that begins with an introduction that asks a question. You may or may not be able to answer the question before the lesson. The question is designed to start you thinking about the idea presented in the essential. You will have a chance at the end of the lesson to look at the question again and expand on your original answer.

- The body of the lesson is designed to resemble an outline. Key concepts are described by numbered titles that are written in the form of a question. The question is then answered in the paragraphs that follow.

- Key vocabulary terms are shown in boldface type when they first appear in the lesson. You will find the definition of each key term in the same paragraph where it first appears.

- The Introduction and Key Concepts is an outline of the key concepts for each essential and is, therefore, written in a straightforward manner. The information is intended to supplement or reinforce concepts that you have already learned.

Summary of Key Concepts

- The Summary of Key Concepts asks you to read the answer to the question you were asked at the beginning of the essential. You then have a chance to change or add to your answer using what you have learned in the essential.

- The Summary of Key Concepts also condenses the information presented in each section of the Introduction and Key Concepts. The summary is organized according to the outline in the Introduction and Key Concepts, and therefore serves as an overview of the essential.

Reviewing Key Terms

- The Reviewing Key Terms is a review of the key terms that are presented in the essential.

- Completing the Reviewing Key Terms exercise helps you become more confident with the terms in the essential.

Assess Your Knowledge

- The Assess Your Knowledge section of the *ChemGuide* serves as a tool for finding out what you have learned in the essential. This section consists of multiple-choice questions that test your knowledge of the key concepts in the essential.

- The questions of the Assess Your Knowledge section are designed to resemble those in state- or district-wide end-of-course examinations. This format will help familiarize you with such examinations.

Math Refresher

- The first section of the Math Refresher summarizes important concepts in mathematics. The topics are arranged in alphabetical order. Each topic includes an example of a solved problem.

- The second section includes problems that give you practice using your math skills to solve problems in chemistry. This section includes topics from chemistry arranged in alphabetical order. Each topic shows you how to analyze, plan, solve, and evaluate a particular type of problem, then provides you with two additional problems to solve on your own.

Final Assessment

- Like the Assessing Knowledge section, the Final Assessment is designed to resemble a chemistry end-of-course examination.

- Whether you take a state end-of-course examination or simply a class final, the Final Assessment serves as an excellent practice examination.

Glossary

- The Glossary provides definitions of the key vocabulary terms that appear in boldface type in each essential.

Tips on Using the ChemGuide: Essentials of Chemistry

The *ChemGuide* is an outline that consists of ten essentials, or big ideas, in chemistry, along with a description of the common themes of the essentials. The following tips provide some suggestions to help you use the *ChemGuide*.

- Read the first paragraph of each lesson, and write your answer to the question posed in that paragraph on the lines provided. The question is intended to help you use what you already know to start thinking about what will be presented in the essential. Remember that when you answer the question, there are not necessarily right or wrong answers. The value of the questions lies in the thought processes that you must go through in trying to answer the question.

- The essentials are presented in outline format. The outline format will help you organize the information. Each concept in the Introduction and Key Concepts is introduced by a numbered section title that is written in the form of a question. Read the question carefully and then keep it in mind as you read that portion of the outline.

- You may find it helpful to create your own outline using the numbered section titles in the Introduction and Key Concepts. Your outline should include the key terms, phrases, or ideas that answer the question posed in the section title. If you can answer the question posed by each section title, you are on your way to understanding the essential.

- At the beginning of the Summary of Key Concepts page, you are asked to review the answer you gave to the question posed when you began the essential. Review what you wrote when you began the essential, then change or add to your answer based on what you learned in the essential.

- Before reviewing the outline portion of the Summary of Key Concepts, review the outline you created while reading the lesson. You should be able to answer the questions that you posed in the section titles of the Introduction and Key Concepts. Read the Summary of Key Concepts to confirm that you can answer those questions.

- The Reviewing Key Terms section provides a review of the key terms in the lesson. Complete the exercise before moving on to the Assess Your Knowledge section.

- Assess Your Knowledge serves two purposes: It assesses your knowledge of the essential and familiarizes you with a format similar to that of many end-of-course examinations. You may take the assessment to prepare for a test or examination.

- After you have covered a topic in class, use the *ChemGuide* to supplement what you learned in class. The essentials will reinforce what you have learned and prepare you for a test or examination covering the topic.

- You can also use the *ChemGuide* as a tool for mastering concepts. If you are having difficulty mastering a particular concept in the textbook, review that concept in the *ChemGuide*. The outline format of the essentials will help you find and master the concept.

- Before a class final or end-of-course examination, review the essentials and take the Final Assessment. If used in this way, the *ChemGuide* can serve as an excellent review or reinforcement tool at the end of the course or semester.

1. Energy and Matter

Introduction and Key Concepts

Suppose you have two rocks that you are using as paperweights sitting on your desk. One is a shiny black rock and the other is a reddish rock with layers of gray material. What statements can you make about the matter or energy in either of the rocks? Write your statements in the space below.

_____

_____

_____

You will need your response to help you review what you have learned by the end of Essential 1.

1.1 What is energy?

The answer to this question is that **energy** is the capacity to do work or produce heat. **Work** is the capacity to move an object over distance against a resisting force.

The many forms of energy can be grouped into three types: radiant energy, kinetic energy, and potential energy. Sunlight is an example of **radiant energy.** The energy carried by objects in motion, such as a baseball that has just been hit over the bleachers, is called **kinetic energy.** Thermal energy and mechanical energy are types of kinetic energy. The energy that is stored or possessed by objects in a position where they can do work, such as the water behind a dam that can turn the blades of a turbine and produce electricity, is called **potential energy.** Food and fuel have chemical potential energy.

Energy is measured in units called calories (cal). A **calorie** is the amount of heat needed to raise the temperature of 1 gram of water by 1 degree Celsius. The International System of Units (SI) unit of energy is the **joule** (J). One calorie is equal to 4.184 J.

The **law of conservation of energy** states that energy is not created or destroyed in any process. Energy simply changes from one form to another.

1.2 How do scientists measure temperature?

Temperature, a measure of how hot or cold something is, is measured with an instrument called a thermometer. A thermometer consists of two parts—the bulb and the stem. The bulb is a reservoir that contains a liquid, such as colored alcohol or mercury, that expands or contracts as the temperature changes. The body of a thermometer is called the stem. The stem is marked with a scale to make reading the liquid level easy. When the temperature increases, the liquid in the bulb expands and rises in the stem. When the temperature decreases the liquid in the bulb contracts and lowers its level in the stem.

In your home, you probably use a thermometer with a Fahrenheit temperature scale. On that scale, the freezing point of water is 32°F and the boiling point of water is 212°F.

In a science laboratory, you will use a thermometer with a Celsius scale, where the freezing point of water is 0°C and the boiling point of water is 100°C. The Celsius scale is used in most of the world outside the United States.

A third scale, the Kelvin scale, is part of the International System of Units (SI). The zero

1. Energy and Matter (continued)

point on the Kelvin scale is called **absolute zero,** the temperature at which particles of matter have no kinetic energy and, therefore, stop moving. The unit on the Kelvin scale is the kelvin (K). Absolute zero equals −273°C. See the drawing below.

Comparison of Temperatures on Fahrenheit, Celsius, and Kelvin Scales

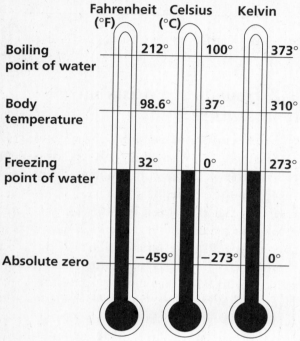

To convert a temperature from Fahrenheit to Celsius, the following formula is used.

$$°C = \tfrac{5}{9} \times (°F - 32)$$

To convert a temperature from Celsius to Fahrenheit, use the following formula.

$$°F = \tfrac{9}{5} °C + 32$$

A change in temperature of 1°F represents only $\tfrac{5}{9}$ as much as a change in temperature of 1°C. In other words, a Celsius degree is $\tfrac{9}{5}$ "larger" than a Fahrenheit degree. However, a kelvin and a Celsius degree are the same "size," and so the formula for converting Celsius degrees to kelvins is simply:

$$K = °C + 273$$

1.3 What is matter?

Matter is anything that has mass (the amount of material in an object) and volume (the space occupied by an object).

Matter on Earth exists in three states—**solid, liquid,** and **gas.** In the interior of the sun, there is a fourth state of matter, **plasma.** It is similar to a gas but exists only at high temperatures.

A solid holds a particular shape and has a definite volume. A liquid has a definite volume, but its shape depends on the shape of its container. A gas has neither a definite shape nor a definite volume. A gas expands to the size and shape of its container.

Matter can change from one state to another if heated or cooled enough. Liquid water becomes water vapor (gas) if heated above water's boiling point, and becomes ice (solid) if cooled below water's freezing point. Other types of matter change from one state to another, too. The temperatures at which that happens depends on the kind of matter.

Different kinds of matter have different characteristics, or properties. A **physical property** of a substance can be observed without changing the identity of the substance. Color and density are examples of physical properties. The characteristics of a substance that cannot be observed without changing the substance are called **chemical properties.** Burning and rusting are chemical properties.

Matter may undergo physical or chemical changes. A change in appearance or state is a physical change. Ice melting into water is an example of a physical change. A chemical change occurs because the identity of the substance changes—from wood to ashes, for example. Whenever matter changes, energy is used or produced.

Like energy, matter is not created or destroyed in any process. This principle is the **law of conservation of matter.**

1. Energy and Matter (continued)

1.4 What units make up matter?

A substance that cannot be separated into simpler substances by a chemical change is called an **element.** Oxygen, gold, and silicon are elements that you may already know. In chemistry, each element is given a symbol (such as O for oxygen, Au for gold, and Si for silicon). These symbols are used in the periodic table, which organizes all the elements according to their properties.

When two or more elements combine in a chemical reaction, they form a new substance called a **compound.** The elements in a given compound are always present in the same proportions. The chemical formula for the compound water is H_2O.

Both elements and compounds are called **pure substances** because each element or compound has a unique set of physical and chemical properties. Minerals, for example, are pure substances. Some minerals such as gold are elements; others such as quartz are compounds.

To identify a substance as an element or a compound, chemists may use a technique called electrolysis. During electrolysis, an electric current is passed through the substance. If the substance is a compound, it will break down into the elements that make it up.

1.5 How do mixtures and pure substances differ?

A **mixture** is a blend of two or more pure substances, and it can be separated into those substances. For example, milk from a cow is a mixture; it separates naturally into cream and skim milk. Also, because each mineral in a rock may have a different color and texture, rocks are mixtures of different minerals.

A mixture having obviously different parts, such as granite, is called a **heterogeneous mixture.** If a mixture looks the same throughout, such as lava, it is a **homogeneous mixture.** Homogeneous mixtures are also called **solutions.**

Several methods of separating mixtures are used. For heterogeneous mixtures, it is fairly easy to use filters or other mechanical "separators." For homogeneous mixtures, special techniques, such as distillation, crystallization, and chromatography, must be used.

1. Summary of Key Concepts

At the beginning of Essential 1, you were asked to make statements about the matter or energy in two rocks. Look at those statements again. In the space below, write how you would change your original statements before you review the key concepts below.

_____

_____

_____

_____

1.1 Energy is the capacity to do work or produce heat. Three basic types of energy are radiant energy, kinetic energy, and potential energy. Energy is neither created nor destroyed in any process. This principle is known as the law of conservation of energy. Similarly, the law of conservation of matter states that matter is neither created nor destroyed in any process.

1.2 Temperature is a measure of how hot or cold something is. Temperature can be measured in degrees Fahrenheit, Celsius, or Kelvin. On the Kelvin scale, the unit is the Kelvin (the SI unit of temperature), and the zero point is called absolute zero.

1.3 Matter is anything having mass and volume. Solid, liquid, gas, and plasma are the four states of matter. All kinds of matter have characteristic physical and chemical properties.

1.4 Elements are substances that cannot be changed into simpler substances by a chemical change. Compounds contain two or more elements combined in a fixed proportion.

1.5 Elements and compounds are pure substances. A blend of two or more pure substances is a mixture. Heterogeneous mixtures are composed of obviously different parts. Homogeneous mixtures appear the same throughout. A solution is a homogeneous mixture.

1. Summary of Key Concepts (continued)

Review Key Terms

On the line provided, write the term from the list that matches each description.

absolute zero   homogeneous mixture   mixture
chemical change   joule   physical change
chemical property   Kelvin scale   physical property
compound   kinetic energy   potential energy
element   law of conservation of energy   pure substance
energy   law of conservation of matter   solid
gas   liquid
heterogeneous mixture   matter

_____ 1. principle that energy can be neither created nor destroyed

_____ 2. involves only mechanical action

_____ 3. can be broken down into simpler substance only by chemical means

_____ 4. can be separated by filtration

_____ 5. used to indicate temperature in the SI system

_____ 6. has definite volume, but shape depends on its container

_____ 7. simplest type of pure substance

_____ 8. basic unit of energy in the SI system

_____ 9. color and density

_____ 10. cannot be observed without altering a substance chemically

_____ 11. principle that matter can be neither created nor destroyed

_____ 12. involves chemical action

_____ 13. blend of pure substances

_____ 14. has both volume and mass

_____ 15. has definite volume and shape

_____ 16. exhibited by a moving object

_____ 17. capacity to do work or cause change

_____ 18. can be observed without altering a substance chemically

_____ 19. made of one kind of material with definite physical and chemical properties

_____ 20. has neither definite volume nor definite shape

_____ 21. the temperature where all movement within a substance stops

_____ 22. stored energy

1. Summary of Key Concepts (continued)

Assess Your Knowledge

Circle the letter of the answer that best completes the sentence or answers the question.

1. The energy in a tightly wound spring is an example of
   a. kinetic energy.
   b. radiant energy.
   c. potential energy.
   d. chemical energy.

2. The SI unit of energy is the
   a. calorie.
   b. joule.
   c. Celsius.
   d. Kelvin.

3. At 85°C, water is in the _____ state.
   a. liquid
   b. gas
   c. elementary
   d. solid

4. Which of the following was caused by a chemical change?
   a. crushed can
   b. melted ice cream
   c. strained tea leaves
   d. rusted nails

5. Which is a pure substance?
   a. hydrogen
   b. milk
   c. a grainy rock
   d. air

6. Which is an example of a physical property?
   a. flammability
   b. color
   c. ability to react with water
   d. browning of a cake as it is baked

2. Atomic Structure and Bonding

Introduction and Key Concepts

Looking up at the sky on a clear night, you see the reddish planet Mars. Other planets and stars may appear bluish-white or yellowish. How can you explain their colors in connection with chemistry? Write your statements in the space below.

_____

_____

_____

_____

You will need your response to help you review what you have learned by the end of Essential 2.

2.1 What have scientists discovered about atomic structure?

Since about 450 B.C. many scientists have believed that small, indivisible particles called **atoms** make up everything in the world. An atom is the smallest portion of an element that retains that element's identity.

According to the **law of constant composition,** a compound always contains elements in the same proportions by mass. This law, together with the idea of atoms, became Dalton's **atomic theory of matter.** Dalton's theory was based on the following postulates:

- Each element is made of extremely small particles called atoms.
- All atoms of each given element are identical to the other atoms of that element, but they differ from atoms of other elements.
- In any chemical reaction, atoms are neither created nor destroyed.
- A given compound always has the same kinds and the same relative numbers of atoms.

There are about 100 different elements, each with its unique kind of atom. "Silhouettes" of atoms can actually be seen by using the scanning tunneling microscope.

In the seventeenth and eighteenth centuries, experiments with electricity showed that atoms are not solid balls, but are made up of charged particles. The first atomic particle studied was the negatively charged **electron.** Twentieth-century experiments with radiation showed there were other particles in the atom.

2.2 What is the current picture of the atom?

Today we know that atoms are made of **protons** and **neutrons** in addition to **electrons.** An atom is mostly empty space. Protons and neutrons are found in the small **nucleus** (center) of the atom, and electrons are found in the space around the nucleus.

- Protons have a positive charge. A proton's mass is expressed as one **atomic mass unit.**
- Electrons have a negative charge. An electron's mass is expressed as zero atomic mass units.
- Neutrons have no charge. A neutron's mass is expressed as one atomic mass unit.

Electrons move around the nucleus, but not in definite orbits like planets circling the sun. In fact, you cannot tell exactly where an electron is at any given time.

2. Atomic Structure and Bonding (continued)

The reason each element's atoms are unique is that each atom has a unique number of protons, called its **atomic number.** Whatever the number of protons in an atom, it has an equal number of electrons, because the positive and negative charges must be equal. The number of neutrons can vary. The number of protons plus neutrons in an atom is indicated by the **mass number.**

Two atoms of the same element that have different numbers of neutrons are called **isotopes.** An isotope's name is written as the element name followed by a hyphen and the mass number, such as chlorine-37. An atomic symbol for an isotope is shown with its atomic and mass numbers. For example, $^{37}_{17}Cl$ is the symbol for chlorine-37. It shows that the atomic number is 17, and the mass number is 37.

In the natural world, there are different isotopes of each element. One isotope may be much more abundant than other isotopes, though. To determine the **atomic mass** of an element, you average the masses of its isotopes, in proportion to their abundance.

If an atom gains or loses electrons, the atom becomes negatively or positively charged and is called an **ion.** The charge of an ion is determined by subtracting the number of electrons from the number of protons. An ion is shown as the atomic symbol with the positive or negative charge at the right, such as Hg^{2+} for an ion of mercury.

2.3 Is light a particle or a wave?

Light is radiant energy, and one form of **electromagnetic radiation.** All radiation is part of the electromagnetic spectrum, from long-wavelength radio waves to short-wavelength cosmic rays. Some other forms of electromagnetic radiation are X-rays, radio waves, and gamma rays. The part of this spectrum we can see is called the **visible spectrum.** The visible spectrum is the small portion of the electromagnetic spectrum that can be seen with the unaided eye. It includes the colors red, orange, yellow, green, blue, indigo, and red. The different colors of visible light correspond to different wavelengths and, therefore, different frequencies. Violet has the shortest wavelength and the highest frequency. Red has the longest wavelength and the lowest frequency.

For hundreds of years, scientists thought light was a beam of wave energy moving through space. In the twentieth century they discovered that light sometimes behaved like a stream of particles. Today light is considered to have properties of both waves and particles. Particles that behave like waves are called **matter waves.**

All waves have four characteristics:
- **amplitude**—wave height measured from the origin to its crest, or peak
- **speed**—3.00×10^8 meters/second for light, c
- **wavelength**—distance between successive crests, λ
- **frequency**—how fast the wave moves up and down, v

The relationship between wavelength and frequency for light is

$$\lambda = c/v$$

Atoms can absorb energy in the form of heat and emit energy in the form of light. Energy is absorbed or released from atoms in pieces of energy called quanta (singular: quantum). A quantum of light is called a **photon.** Atoms of each element release photons when they absorb energy or become excited. When an atom becomes excited, electrons move into a higher energy state or orbital. Then, as they return to their normal orbital, they release energy in the form of light.

2. Atomic Structure and Bonding (continued)

2.4 Where are electrons found in an atom?

Orbitals, or areas where an electron with a given energy is likely to be found, surround an atomic nucleus. An orbital is not precise, like a planetary orbit. It is more like a fuzzy sphere or dumbbell. Each orbital can contain a maximum of 2 electrons.

Orbitals are divided into the sublevels, which may be labeled *s*, *p*, *d*, and *f*. The main or **principal energy level** is designated by the quantum number such as 1, 2, or 3. The number of sublevels equals the number for that energy level; energy level 3 ($n = 3$), for instance, has 3 sublevels. Energy level 1 is nearest the nucleus, and energy level 2 is farther away from the nucleus. Within each level, the sublevels are like concentric spheres, with sublevel *s* being nearest the nucleus. The *p* orbitals are arranged at right angles to each other within their sublevel.

In each energy level, the maximum number of electrons depends on the number and type of sublevels it contains. Sublevel *s* contains only one orbital, and so it can contain only 2 electrons. The table below shows the pattern of electron distributions in the various levels.

Can you see a numerical pattern from one level to the next?

The highest energy level for any atom is the level farthest from the nucleus. As you might expect, that is also true for the sublevels. An electron in sublevel 3*d*, for instance, has more energy than one in sublevel 3*p*. When an atom absorbs energy, an electron can jump from one orbital to the next outer orbital. When the atom emits energy, the electron jumps inward.

The distribution of electrons in an atom's orbitals is called the **electron configuration** of the atom. To determine the electron configuration for an atom, you need to start with the atomic number, which equals the number of protons. As the number of protons and electrons must be equal, the atomic number also gives you the number of electrons. You can fill out a chart filling each energy level and sublevel in order until you have accounted for all the electrons.

If you could magnify and look at two atoms for comparison, you would see their "surface" characteristics. One might have a single electron in the outermost sublevel, and the other might have two electrons there. Even though the atoms would look similar, the difference of one electron is great because the electrons of the outermost orbital are the ones available to react with other atoms.

Summary of Energy Levels, Sublevels, and Orbitals

Principal Energy Level	Maximum Total Number of Electrons in Level	Sublevels	Orbitals in Each Sublevel	Number of Electrons in Orbitals (at 2 per orbital)
$n = 1$	2	1*s*	1	2
$n = 2$	8	2*s*, 2*p*	1, 3	2, 6
$n = 3$	18	3*s*, 3*p*, 3*d*	1, 3, 5	2, 6, 10
$n = 4$	32	4*s*, 4*p*, 4*d*, 4*f*	1, 3, 5, 7	2, 6, 10, 14

2. Atomic Structure and Bonding (continued)

2.5 What does the periodic table show?

When you study the **periodic table** of elements, you can see that the elements' physical and chemical properties show a repeating pattern known as the **periodic law.** Some periodic tables contain more information than others, but every square in any periodic table will show at least the following:

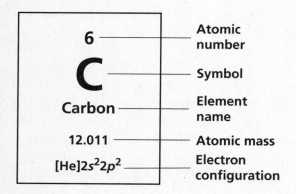

The number at the top is the atomic number. The letter is the element's chemical symbol, and is shown just above the element's name. Below the name is the atomic mass. As the diagram of the atom shows, the mass number of carbon-12 is exactly 12 (6 protons and 6 neutrons). The atomic mass is slightly more than that because there are some heavier isotopes of carbon in nature, which increases the average mass.

Our current periodic table has 112 squares, one for each known element. They are arranged in 18 vertical columns called **groups,** or **families,** and in 7 horizontal rows called **periods.** The first period has only two elements, hydrogen and helium. As you move down the table, the periods contain more elements. As you move across the table from left to right, the atomic number of each element increases.

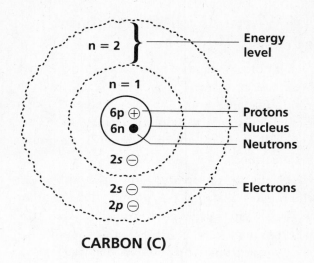

CARBON (C)

Some of the periodic trends you can see in the table are:

- The **atomic radius,** which is the distance from the center of the nucleus to the outermost electron, increases as you move downward, and decreases as you move from left to right. This is because atoms with larger atomic numbers have more energy levels of electrons.
- An atom's **ionization energy,** which is the energy needed to remove one of its electrons, decreases as you move downward, and increases as you move from left to right. This follows from the previous trend, because electrons are held more tightly in atoms with small atomic radii.
- An atom's **electron affinity,** which is the attraction for an extra electron, increases from left to right.

2. Atomic Structure and Bonding (continued)

2.6 What are the major groups of elements?

If you look at the periodic table on pages 137 and 138 of this book, you will see that it contains three major groups of elements. These are the **metals, semimetals,** and **nonmetals.** In general, these elements are arranged from left to right. There is one exception, however. Hydrogen is a unique element and not part of any group. Therefore, it is placed at the top left of the table.

Metals, in general, are good conductors of heat and electricity, are shiny, and are solids at room temperature. Most are malleable, meaning they can be hammered into thin sheets (such as aluminum foil). Many are ductile, meaning they can be drawn out into wire.

Elements that do not have the characteristics of metals are, of course, nonmetals. Semimetals, or metalloids, have properties that are intermediate between those of metals and nonmetals.

Each of the columns in the periodic table contains a group of elements that all have the same number of electrons in the outer shell. These outer electrons are called **valence electrons,** and they account for the properties of elements in that group. In column 1 (1A, IA), for instance, each element has just one valence electron. This group is called the **alkali metals.** Column 2 (2A, IIA) elements each have two valence electrons. They are the **alkaline earth metals.** Skipping across to the right side of the table, the elements in column 17 (7A, VIIA), the **halogens,** have 7 valence electrons. Finally, column 18 (VIIIA, 8A) contains the **noble gases.** These four groups are often referred to as families—the alkali metals family, for instance, because they are closely related in structure and properties.

Atoms tend to gain, lose, or share electrons to acquire a set of 8 valence electrons. Because *oct-* means 8, this principle is called the octet rule. Oxygen, for example, has 6 valence electrons, and tends to gain 2 more from another atom or group of atoms. Because each electron it gains has a 1− charge, the oxygen ion formed in that way has a 2− charge (shown as O^{2-}). Sodium, with one valence electron, tends to lose it to another atom or group of atoms. Because the electron lost has a 1− charge, the sodium ion formed in that way has a 1+ charge (shown as Na^{1+}).

The elements at the top right tend to attract electrons more strongly than other elements do; in other words, they have a high **electronegativity.** The least electronegative, and most reactive, metals are those in the first two columns, the alkali metal and alkaline earth-metal families. That is because the one or two valence electrons of those atoms are easily transferred to other atoms. In fact, alkali metals are never found as free elements in nature; they are always found combined with other elements, in compounds.

The alkali metals have all the properties of other metals. Also, they have low densities and low melting points. Sodium and potassium are the most abundant alkali metals.

Elements in the second column of the periodic table, the alkaline earth metals, include calcium and magnesium. Alkaline earth metals are reactive, but not quite so reactive as the alkali metals are. Also, their densities and melting points are a little higher than the alkali metals' are. They are found in compounds rather than the elemental state. The most abundant of these elements, calcium and magnesium, occur widely in mineral deposits such as limestone ($CaCO_3$) and magnesite ($MgCO_3$).

Metals in columns to the right of the alkaline earth metals have properties indicating their positions in the periodic table. Many, such as iron, silver, gold, and lead, are familiar to you, because they are used in building materials, jewelry, and coins. Most of these metals have

2. Atomic Structure and Bonding (continued)

high densities and melting points. Some are radioactive.

The semimetals are the diagonally arranged group of elements that divide the metals from the nonmetals in the periodic. One of these elements is silicon (Si), the semimetal used in computer chips and in glass.

The remaining elements are the nonmetals. These include elements that are important in living organisms, such as nitrogen, oxygen, and phosphorus. Within the nonmetals are smaller families such as the halogens and noble gases. Halogens (column 17) are found in nature as two-atom **molecules,** or combined atoms—F_2 (fluorine), Cl_2 (chlorine), and I_2 (iodine), for example. Having 7 valence electrons, they are extremely reactive. The noble gases (column 18) already have 8 valence electrons, and so they are extremely unreactive. Examples of noble gases are helium (He) and neon (Ne).

Although hydrogen (H) is at the top left of most periodic tables, it is a nonmetal. Under normal conditions it is a colorless, odorless gas. On Earth, most hydrogen is combined with oxygen in the form of water (H_2O). Hydrogen is the most abundant element in the universe.

2. Summary of Key Concepts

At the beginning of Essential 2, you were asked if you could make any statements about the chemistry and colors of astronomical objects. Look at what you wrote. Are you able to better answer the question? Write how you would change your original statements before you review the key concepts below.

_____

_____

_____

2.1 According to the atomic theory of matter, atoms are the smallest particles of an element retaining the element's identity, and all atoms in an element are identical. In chemical reactions, atoms are neither created not destroyed. According to the law of constant composition, compounds always have the same kinds and relative numbers of each atom.

2.2 Over 100 atoms combine to form all kinds of matter. Atoms contain electrically charged particles called protons (positive) and electrons (negative), and uncharged particles called neutrons. An atomic nucleus contains protons and may contain neutrons. Electrons move in the space around the nucleus. The number of protons in an atom's nucleus is its atomic number. The number of protons plus neutrons is its mass number. An ion is an atom or group of atoms having a net electrical charge. Different isotopes of an element have the same number of protons in their atoms, but differing numbers of neutrons.

2.3 The electromagnetic spectrum spans a wide range of wavelengths, from radio waves to X-rays. Light is the form of electromagnetic radiation that makes up the visible spectrum. It may act as either waves or particles; its behavior is described as matter waves. Like other waves, amplitude, speed, wavelength, and frequency define matter waves. Energy from matter waves is absorbed by or released from atoms in the form of photons.

2.4 The arrangement of electrons around the nucleus is the electron configuration. The atoms are arranged in sublevels whose number corresponds to the principal energy level. The region around an atom's nucleus where an electron having a particular amount of energy will probably be found is called an orbital.

2.5 According to the periodic law, when the elements are arranged in order of increasing atomic number, their properties show a periodic pattern. An element's electronegativity indicates its attraction for electrons in a chemical bond.

2.6 Atoms tend to gain, lose, or share electrons to acquire a set of 8 valence electrons. Because the alkali metals are all very reactive, they do not exist as free elements in nature. They form ions with a 1+ charge. The alkaline earth metals are a little less reactive, and form ions with a 2+ charge. The columns farthest to the right of the periodic table are the very reactive halogens (column 17) and the least reactive noble gases (column 18). Hydrogen has unique characteristics, and is a nonmetal though it is at the top of column 1, the farthest column to the left on the periodic table. It is the most abundant element in the universe.

2. Summary of Key Concepts (continued)

Review Key Terms

On the line provided, write the term from the list that matches each description.

alkali metal   electron configuration   mass number   periodic law
alkaline earth metal   electronegativity   metal   photon
atom   group   neutron   proton
atomic mass   halogen   noble gases   semimetal
atomic number   ion   nonmetal   valence electron
electron   isotope   period   wavelength

_____ **1.** element found in Column 2 in the periodic table

_____ **2.** has characteristics of both metals and nonmetals

_____ **3.** number of protons in an atom of an element

_____ **4.** number of protons plus neutrons

_____ **5.** column in the periodic table

_____ **6.** strength of attraction of electrons in a chemical bond

_____ **7.** element that is ductile and conducts electricity

_____ **8.** has different number of neutrons but same number of protons

_____ **9.** element that is not a metal

_____ **10.** electron in outermost orbital

_____ **11.** charged atom

_____ **12.** average mass of the element's isotopes

_____ **13.** negatively charged atomic particle

_____ **14.** quantum of electromagnetic energy

_____ **15.** family in which sodium or potassium appear

_____ **16.** Column 17 of the periodic table

_____ **17.** positively charged atomic particle

_____ **18.** distribution of electrons in an atom's orbitals

_____ **19.** distance from crest to crest

_____ **20.** uncharged atomic particle

_____ **21.** states that the physical and chemical properties of elements show a repeating trend

_____ **22.** small, indivisible particle

_____ **23.** least reactive family in the periodic table

_____ **24.** row in the periodic table

2. Summary of Key Concepts (continued)

Assess Your Knowledge

Circle the letter of the answer that best completes the sentence or answers the question.

1. The number of protons and neutrons in an atom is indicated by its
    a. atomic number.
    b. atomic mass unit.
    c. mass number.
    d. isotope.

2. A negative charge will
    a. repel another negative charge.
    b. not affect a positive charge.
    c. attract another negative charge.
    d. repel a positive charge.

3. Isotopes of the same element contain the same number of
    a. atomic masses.
    b. nuclei.
    c. neutrons.
    d. protons.

4. Which of the following is not a characteristic of waves?
    a. amplitude
    b. direction
    c. frequency
    d. speed

5. Which of the following is not one of the periodic trends?
    a. electron affinity
    b. ionization energy
    c. number of isotopes
    d. atomic radius

6. Which electron transition is associated with absorption of energy?
    a. $3p$ to $3s$
    b. $4p$ to $3p$
    c. $3p$ to $2s$
    d. $3s$ to $3p$

7. The energy of an atom in an excited state is _____ its energy in the ground state.
    a. less than
    b. equal to
    c. independent of
    d. greater than

2. Summary of Key Concepts (continued)

8. How many electrons can an orbital have?
   a. 2
   b. 8
   c. 1
   d. 0

9. The elements in Group 1A (IA, or column 1), at the far left of the periodic table, are called
   a. alkaline earth metals.
   b. halogens.
   c. noble gases.
   d. alkali metals.

10. An atom's attraction for an added electron is called its
    a. ionization energy.
    b. electron affinity.
    c. electronegativity.
    d. atomic radius.

11. Which element is an alkaline earth metal?
    a. sodium
    b. chlorine
    c. magnesium
    d. oxygen

12. A malleable, shiny substance is most likely a
    a. metal.
    b. nonmetal.
    c. noble gas.
    d. semimetal.

13. Which element is the most abundant element in the universe?
    a. silicon
    b. oxygen
    c. hydrogen
    d. nitrogen

14. The alkaline earth metals are
    a. more reactive than the alkali metals.
    b. less reactive than the semimetals.
    c. less reactive than the noble gases.
    d. less reactive than alkali metals.

3. Chemical Reactions

Introduction and Key Concepts

Think of three examples from everyday life of substances reacting to produce different substances. What do you think happens to the atoms in these reactions? Write your ideas in the space below.

_____

_____

_____

_____

You will need your response to help you review what you have learned by the end of Essential 3.

3.1 How do ions bond to one another?

When an atom loses or gains one or more of its electrons (usually its outermost, or valence, electrons) it acquires a net electrical charge, and is called an ion. A positive ion is called a **cation;** and a negative ion, an **anion.** Because unlike charges attract each other, a cation and an anion will cling to each other to form an **ionic bond.** An example is the bond between a metal cation and a nonmetal anion. The compound formed in this way is called an **ionic compound.** Sodium chloride, NaCl, is an ionic compound.

Atoms tend to gain, lose, or share electrons in order to acquire a full set of valence electrons, which for most atoms is 8. This is called the **octet rule,** and is one of the most important rules in chemistry.

Because of the octet rule, sodium, with one valence electron, tends to lose it to another atom or group of atoms. As the electron lost has a 1– charge, the sodium ion formed in that way has a 1+ charge, shown as Na^{1+}. Similarly, chlorine tends to gain an electron to become a Cl^{1-} ion. The ions of sodium and chlorine are strongly attracted to each other, forming an ionic compound and releasing energy. Both ions now have 8 valence electrons, as if they were noble gas atoms, and are very stable. Some elements in the center of the periodic table do not follow the octet rule, but most of the others do.

As an easy way of showing valence electrons of an atom or ion, chemists use Lewis dot diagrams, such as these:

Chlorine ion, Cl^{1-}   **Chlorine atom, Cl**

Ions can be **monatomic,** consisting of one atom, or **polyatomic,** consisting of two or more atoms. The chlorine ion is monatomic. A polyatomic ion is a group of atoms that act together as one ion, such as the sulfate ion, SO_4^{2-}.

When the ions of only two elements form a compound, a **binary ionic compound** forms. These compounds are named for their cation and anion, in that order, such as sodium chloride for NaCl. When more than two elements are involved, the formula includes numbers to show the ratios in the compound. For example, aluminum oxide is shown as Al_2O_3; for every 2 aluminum ions in the compound, there are 3 oxide ions. This formula is called an **empirical formula.** An empirical formula is the chemical formula that gives the simplest whole-number ratio of atoms of elements in a compound instead of the actual number of atoms in the compound.

3. Chemical Reactions *(continued)*

Any ionic compound is electrically neutral, so that the total of positive charges equals the total of negative charges. For example, in Al_2O_3 each Al^{3+} has a charge of $3+$, so the total positive charge is 6. Each O^{2-} has a charge of $2-$, so the total negative charge is also 6. Notice that in an empirical formula, you are dealing with ratios. You do not know how many actual ions are involved.

Some atoms may form ions with different charges. When a copper atom loses one electron, it becomes Cu^{1+}, or $Cu(I)$. If it loses two, it becomes Cu^{2+}, or $Cu(II)$.

3.2 What is covalent bonding?

When an ionic compound is formed, electrons are transferred from one ion to another. Another type of compound, called a **molecule,** is formed when atoms share electrons. This sharing is called **covalent bonding.** As in ionic compounds, the atoms in molecules obey the octet rule. For example, two atoms that each have 7 valence electrons can share electrons so that each one has the "use" of 8. A Lewis dot formula shows the sharing in this way:

$$:\overset{\displaystyle\cdot\cdot}{\underset{\displaystyle\cdot\cdot}{Cl}}:\overset{\displaystyle\cdot\cdot}{\underset{\displaystyle\cdot\cdot}{Cl}}:$$

A molecule of chlorine (Cl₂)

Substances made of molecules are called **molecular substances.** Some molecules contain only two atoms, while others may contain thousands. The atoms in a molecule may be from the same element or different elements.

You can write an empirical formula to show the ratio of atoms in a molecule, just as you can for an ionic compound. The empirical formula for the simple sugar glucose is CH_2O. But a molecule of glucose actually contains more atoms. To show all the atoms in a molecule of glucose, the **molecular formula** is written as $C_6H_{12}O_6$. A **structural formula** gives even more

detail, showing how the atoms are arranged and bonded to each other. In a structural formula, a pair of shared electrons is shown by 2 Lewis dots or by a dash representing a **single covalent bond.** Thus, the Cl_2 molecule would be shown as Cl—Cl.

Two atoms may share more than one pair of electrons. Each pair they share is shown by 2 Lewis dots or by a dash. The O_2 molecule is shown as O=O, because 2 pairs (4 electrons) are shared between the two atoms. The $=$ represents a **double covalent bond.** There are even triple covalent bonds in some molecules. Any atom in a molecule may have some electrons that are shared with other atoms, and others that are unshared.

Atoms toward the bottom of the periodic table form longer bonds with each other than atoms closer to the top, because their larger atomic radii lessen the attraction between their nuclei and the electrons in the bonds. Multiple bonds between atoms are stronger and shorter than single bonds between atoms because multiple bonds have more electrons to "glue" the positively charged nuclei together.

3.3 How do compounds get their names?

Compounds are named for their atoms and bonds. Sometimes the name is obvious, as in sodium chloride, NaCl. Other times, you have to analyze the formula and figure out the name. To name an ionic compound, name the cation first, indicating its valence. For example, in the compound $Cu(NO_3)_2$, the valence of NO_3 (nitrate) is $1-$. If two nitrate ions are needed to balance each Cu ion, then the valence of the Cu ion must be $2+$ or (II). Thus, this compound is called copper(II) nitrate. Naming molecular compounds is similar; you name the less electronegative atoms first.

Ionic compounds may absorb water into their structures, forming substances called

3. Chemical Reactions (continued)

hydrates. An example of a hydrate is copper(II) sulfate pentahydrate, $CuSO_4 \cdot 5H_2O$. When no water is present in the compound, it is called **anhydrous** copper(II) sulfate.

Molecular substances that dissolve in water to produce hydrogen ions (H^{1+}) are **acids.** Acids are named for their anions; for example, H_2SO_4, sulfuric acid, is formed from a sulfate. If the anion's name ends in *-ide*, then the prefix *hydro-* begins the acid name. For example, Cl^{1-} is *chloride* and HCl is *hydrochloric acid*.

Because of the law of conservation of mass, the total amount of reactants must equal the total amount of products. Also, the number of atoms of each element to the left of the arrow must equal the number of atoms of that element to the right of the arrow. For the reaction between magnesium metal and nitrogen gas that forms magnesium nitride, the equation is written:

$$Mg + N_2 \rightarrow Mg_3N_2$$

There are two atoms of nitrogen on each side, but the magnesium atoms are not balanced. There is 1 magnesium atom on the left and 3 magnesium atoms on the right. To balance the number of atoms, you need to add the coefficient 3 before the magnesium on the reactant side of the equation. Now the chemical equation is balanced. There are 3 magnesium atoms on each side of the equation, and 2 nitrogen atoms on each side of the equation.

Here is a more difficult equation to be balanced:

$$Al_2(SO_4)_3 + BaCl_2 \rightarrow AlCl_3 + BaSO_4$$

Only the barium atoms are balanced. While balancing equations is largely a matter of trial and error, you will find with practice that usually it is better to leave balancing oxygen and hydrogen atoms to the last. So, you might start with aluminum:

$$Al_2(SO_4)_3 + BaCl_2 \rightarrow 2\ AlCl_3 + BaSO_4$$

There are 2 chlorine atoms on the left and 6 on the right. To correct that, add the coefficient 3 before barium chloride:

$$Al_2(SO_4)_3 + 3\ BaCl_2 \rightarrow 2\ AlCl_3 + BaSO_4$$

Now, there are 3 each of sulfate ions and barium atoms on the left, but only 1 of each on the right. Make one more correction by adding a coefficient of 3 in front of barium sulfate, and the equation is balanced:

$$Al_2(SO_4)_3 + 3\ BaCl_2 \rightarrow 2\ AlCl_3 + 3\ BaSO_4$$

3.4 What shapes do molecules have?

Molecules come in a variety of shapes, and their shapes play an important role in determining a molecule's properties. According to the **VSEPR (valence-shell electron pair repulsion) theory,** pairs of valence electrons are arranged as far from each other as possible. The repulsion force between electrons is what gives rise to the shape of molecules.

Molecules may be linear (straight); trigonal planar (flat and triangular); tetrahedral (having four surfaces), pyramidal (shaped like a pyramid), and bent. Each of these shapes has characteristic **bond angles.** These angles are associated with **hybrid orbitals.** When atoms bond, their *s* and *p* orbitals can mix to form *sp* orbitals (in linear molecules), sp^2 (trigonal planar), or sp^3 (tetrahedral).

Ball-and-Stick Model of Methane, CH₄

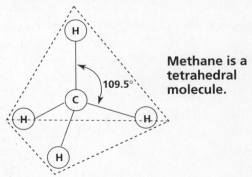

Methane is a tetrahedral molecule.

The molecule's shape may be shown with printed formulas or with **ball-and-stick models.** Ball-and-stick models, such as the one above, are three-dimensional physical models in which

3. Chemical Reactions (continued)

atoms are represented by balls, and bonds are represented by sticks.

3.5 What is molecular polarity?

If the electrons shared by two atoms are pulled more to one atom than the other, that part of the molecule is slightly more negatively charged, and the molecule is said to be **polar.** Polarity occurs when one atom is more electronegative than the other. This is shown by the Greek letter delta, δ. The more negative "pole" of the molecule is labeled with a δ^-; the more positive part, with a δ^+. If neither atom is more electronegative than the other, the molecule is **nonpolar.** For example, when both atoms are of the same element, such as in oxygen gas, the molecule is nonpolar.

A polar molecule, or **dipole,** has one positively charged and one negatively charged end. The shape of a molecule and the polarity of its bonds together determine whether the molecule is polar or nonpolar. When a compound consists of polar molecules, the positive and negative poles of different molecules are attracted to each other. This explains some properties of water, for instance.

3.6 What is a chemical reaction?

A **chemical reaction** is what happens when substances are converted into new substances with different physical and chemical properties. Usually atoms bond to satisfy the octet rule, which increases their stability. During a chemical reaction the number and type of atoms is the same on each side of the equation. The atoms may be combined differently, but the actual number of each type of atom is the same.

Reactions shown in this form are chemical equations. The letters may be given as word (word equations) or as chemical formulas (formula equations). The substances to the left of the arrows are the **reactants;** those to the right are the **products.**

3.7 How are chemical reactions classified?

The four general types of chemical reactions are direct combination, decomposition, single-replacement, and double-replacement.

By knowing which type of reaction is occurring, you can predict the products to be formed. In a **direct combination reaction,** sometimes called a synthesis reaction, two or more reactants form one product. When calcium burns in oxygen, it forms the compound calcium oxide. The equation for this reaction is written as follows.

$$2\ Ca + O_2 \rightarrow 2\ CaO$$

In a **decomposition reaction** the reaction is just the opposite. A single reactant is broken down into 2 or more products (compounds or elements). When limestone (calcium carbonate) is heated, it breaks down into calcium oxide and carbon dioxide. The equation for this reaction is written as follows.

$$2\ CaCO_3 \rightarrow 2\ CaO + 2\ CO_2$$

In a **single-replacement reaction,** the reactants are always one element and one compound. An example is when magnesium reacts with copper(II) sulfate, releasing copper and forming magnesium sulfate. The equation for this reaction is written as follows.

$$Mg + CuSO_4 \rightarrow MgSO_4 + Cu$$

To determine which metals will replace other metals, you look up the metals involved in an activity series, which lists elements in order of chemical activity. Any metal in the series can replace those lower down in the series.

In a **double-replacement reaction,** each reactant is a compound, and the two parts of each compound are exchanged. Usually the reactants are ionic compounds. An example is the reaction of calcium carbonate with hydrochloric acid. The equation for this reaction is written as follows.

$$CaCO_3 + 2\ HCl \rightarrow CaCl_2 + H_2CO_3$$

3. Chemical Reactions (continued)

3.8 How much is a mole?

To find the mass of chemicals for work in the laboratory, you need to measure them in grams, not in molecules. In order to convert from molecules to grams, you will use a quantity called a **mole.** By looking at the formula of a compound and adding the atomic masses in the proper ratio, you get its total **formula mass.**

A mole of any element is defined as the number of atoms of that element equal to the number of atoms in exactly 12.0 grams of carbon-12. The number of atoms in one mole of atoms is always the same; it is equal to 6.02×10^{23}. Thus, there are 6.02×10^{23} hydrogen atoms in 1.0 gram of hydrogen, 6.02×10^{23} oxygen atoms in 16.0 grams of oxygen, and 6.02×10^{23} copper atoms in 63.5 grams of copper.

The mole establishes a relationship between the atomic mass unit and the gram. The mass in grams of 1 mole of a substance is numerically equal to its atomic mass or formula mass in atomic mass units. This number, 6.02×10^{23}, is known as **Avogadro's number** (abbreviated N). The mass in grams of 1 mole of a substance is called the **molar mass** ($\mathcal{M}$).

In the reaction $2\ Ca + O_2 \rightarrow 2\ CaO$, 2 moles of Ca and 1 mole of O_2 react to form 2 moles of CaO. The atomic mass of Ca is 40 and the atomic mass of O is 16, and so 80 g of Ca react with 32 g of O_2 to yield 112 g of CaO.

The general formula for working with moles is:

number of moles of substance + molar mass (in g)

$\qquad$ = weight of substance (in g)

Therefore,

Ca: 40 amu/atom $\times$ 2 atoms	=	80 amu
O: 16 amu/atom $\times$ 2 atoms	=	32 amu
	Formula mass	=	112 amu
	Molar mass	=	112 g/mol

Because it is difficult to measure the mass of a gas, gases are measured by volume. The **molar volume** of any gas at standard temperature and pressure (STP) is 22.4 L.

The percentage composition of a compound is the percentage by mass of each element in it. To find the percentage composition, divide the mass of each element by the compound's total mass and then multiply by 100%.

The **empirical formula** for a compound can be found by using the percentage composition or by using the mass of each element to find the number of moles. Then the mole ratios are compared. To find the molecular formula of an unknown compound, compare the compound's molar mass with its empirical formula mass. That gives the multiple of the empirical formula that is needed for the molecular formula.

Because ionic substances are made up of ions rather than of separate molecules, they cannot be described using molecular formulas.

3.9 What limits a chemical reaction?

In chemistry, the study of quantitative relationships in formulas and reactions is called **stoichiometry.** It includes the calculations of moles, mass, and volume. It also includes measuring the amounts of reactants and products in chemical reactions.

In setting up a chemical experiment or large-scale industrial process, you may need to figure out how much of each reactant is needed or how much product can be expected. These problems are called **mole-mole problems.** To do them, set up a mole:mole ratio based on a balanced molecular equation. The coefficients in the equation can be read as "moles of." If 2 mol of reactant A requires 3 mol of reactant B to produce 3 mol of product C ($2\ A + 3\ B \rightarrow 3\ C$), set up ratios such as 2:3 and 3:3 (or 1:1), and use them in thinking about problems before performing the calculations.

3. Chemical Reactions *(continued)*

You can set up **mass-mass problems** by using similar ratios and reasoning. If, for example, a certain mass of reactant A is available, calculate how much of B is needed, and how much of C will be produced. Or, to make a certain amount of C, set up another calculation of how much of A and B are needed. It is important to remember that in these problems, the coefficients represent moles, not grams. Be sure to convert the moles to grams.

Because 1 mol of any gas takes up 22.4 L, mole-mole ratios may be used to calculate the volume of gas produced in a reaction. If the reactants are solids or liquids, these are **mass–volume problems.** If both the reactants and products are gases, they are **volume–volume problems.**

In these types of problems, one of the reactants in an equation often limits the amount of product that is formed. That reactant, called the **limiting reactant,** is entirely used up in the reaction; the other reactant will be left over.

The left-over reactant is said to be "in excess." To find out which is the limiting reactant, do a mass–mass problem for each reactant: (1) set up the balanced chemical equation; (2) set up the ratio of reactant to product; and (3) calculate the amount of product, based on that reactant's molar mass. By comparing the amounts of product, the limiting reactant—the one that would produce the smaller amount of product—is identified. (Notice that the limiting reactant is not necessarily the one with the least mass or volume, but rather the one that produces the least product.)

In the chemistry lab, you often get a smaller **yield** of product than expected from an equation. The amount you calculated is called the expected yield. The amount that is experimentally produced is the actual yield. The ratio of the actual yield to the expected yield, multiplied by 100%, is the percent yield.

3. Summary of Key Concepts

At the beginning of Essential 3, you were asked to make statements about what you thought happens to atoms in a chemical reaction. Using what you have learned in this lesson, change or add to your statements before you review the key concepts below.

_____

_____

3.1 A cation and anion are joined by an ionic bond, forming an ionic compound. Usually cations are formed from metals, and anions from nonmetals.

3.2 Atoms are joined by covalent bonds, forming a molecular compound. Both ionic and molecular compounds satisfy the octet rule. Sometimes double or triple bonds are necessary. Empirical formulas show ratios, and molecular and structural formulas show the actual numbers, of atoms. Structural formulas show bonds also. Atoms near the bottom of the periodic table form longer bonds than those near the top do, and single bonds are longer than multiple bonds.

3.3 A compound is named for the atoms or ions composing it. Prefixes and suffixes help indicate the number of atoms of different kinds. A hydrate is an ionic compound that has absorbed water molecules. An acid is a molecule that releases a hydrogen cation and an anion when dissolved in water.

3.4 Molecules have a variety of shapes with characteristic bond angles. The repulsion force between electrons is what gives rise to the shape of molecules.

3.5 If electrons are shared unequally, the bond is polar. Whether the sharing is equal or unequal depends on the electronegativities of the atoms in the compound. A polar molecule has one positively charged, and one negatively charged, end. Polarity affects molecular shape.

3.6 When reactants participate in a chemical reaction, they form products with different physical and chemical properties. Products of chemical reactions are ordinarily more stable than the reactants. The number of atoms of each element on one side of a chemical equation equals the number for that element on the other side.

3.7 Most chemical reactions fall into the general types of combination, decomposition, single-replacement, and double-replacement.

3.8 A mole contains 6.02×10^{23} atoms or molecules of a substance. This is called Avogadro's number. The mass of 1 mole of a substance is its molar mass. The molar volume of a gas is 22.4 L at STP.

3.9 Stoichiometric problems are based on the quantitative relationships among the reactants and products in a chemical reaction. To solve stoichiometric problems, convert the given information to moles, use the molar ratio to determine the number of moles of the reactant or product, and then convert the calculated number of moles to the desired unit for a reactant or product. If one reactant is entirely used up in a reaction it is called the limiting reactant.

3. Summary of Key Concepts (continued)

Review Key Terms

On the line provided, write the term from the list that matches each description.

anhydrous   empirical formula   polar
anion   limiting reactant   polarity
Avogadro's number   molar volume   polyatomic ion
balanced chemical equation   mole   product
covalent bond   molecular formula   reactant
decomposition reaction   octet rule   single covalent bond
double covalent bond   percent yield   stoichiometry

_____ **1.** one pair of shared electrons

_____ **2.** ionic compound containing no water

_____ **3.** negative ion

_____ **4.** ion containing more than one atom

_____ **5.** shows only ratios of elements in molecule

_____ **6.** formed by sharing electrons

_____ **7.** principle that atoms tend to gain, lose, or share electrons until they have 8 valence electrons

_____ **8.** more electronegative in one part

_____ **9.** $C_6H_{12}O_6$, for example

_____ **10.** has 4 shared electrons

_____ **11.** having oppositely charged ends

_____ **12.** on the left side of the arrow in a chemical equation

_____ **13.** formed in a chemical reaction

_____ **14.** or each element, shows equal numbers in the reactants and products

_____ **15.** breakdown of a compound

_____ **16.** atoms or molecules in a mole of substance

_____ **17.** 22.4 L of a gas

_____ **18.** can be defined either as number of particles or as mass in grams

_____ **19.** measurement and calculations of quantitative relationships in chemical reactions

_____ **20.** used up entirely in a reaction

_____ **21.** actual yield : expected yield × 100%

3. *Summary of Key Concepts* (continued)

Assess Your Knowledge

Circle the letter of the answer that best completes the sentence or answers the question.

1. Positively charged ions are called
   a. anions.
   b. polyatomic ions.
   c. cations.
   d. monatomic ions.

2. Hydrates are
   a. ionic compounds that lack any water in their structures.
   b. ionic compounds that have absorbed water into their structures.
   c. molecules that release hydrogen ions when dissolved in water.
   d. molecules in which the atoms have unequal electronegativities.

3. A group of atoms united by covalent bonds is a(n)
   a. ionic compound.
   b. anhydrous compound.
   c. monatomic compound.
   d. molecule.

4. Valence electrons are
   a. shared between atoms in a molecule.
   b. found in the energy level nearest the nucleus.
   c. shared between atoms in an ionic compound.
   d. lost or gained by atoms in an ionic compound.

5. To emphasize the ratios of atoms in a molecule, you would show a(n) _____ formula.
   a. empirical
   b. structural
   c. molecular
   d. nonpolar

6. Cations are usually formed by
   a. nonmetallic elements.
   b. semimetallic elements.
   c. metallic elements.
   d. halogen elements.

3. Summary of Key Concepts (continued)

7. In naming an ionic compound, you would begin with the name of the
   a. more electronegative atom.
   b. anion.
   c. nonmetallic ion.
   d. cation.

8. Which is an example of a polar molecule?
   a. water
   b. oxygen
   c. hydrogen
   d. carbon dioxide

9. Atoms are _____ during a chemical reaction.
   a. synthesized
   b. destroyed
   c. rearranged
   d. unbalanced

10. A double-replacement reaction might be shown as
    a. $A + BX \rightarrow AX + B$.
    b. $NaCl + HOH \rightarrow NaOH + HCl$.
    c. $CaCO_3 \rightarrow CaO + CO_2$.
    d. $O_2 + Mg \rightarrow MgO$.

11. To balance the equation $CO_2 + HOH \rightarrow C_6H_{12}O_6 + O_2$, you might begin by
    a. adding the coefficient 6 before HOH.
    b. changing HOH to H_6OH_6.
    c. adding the coefficient 12 before CO_2.
    d. adding the coefficient 6 before CO_2.

12. The parts of an atom that take part in chemical reactions are its
    a. valence electrons.
    b. positively charged poles.
    c. inner-shell electrons.
    d. protons and neutrons.

13. The mass of 2 mol of oxygen gas (O_2) is
    a. 44.8 L.
    b. 44.8 g.
    c. 64 g.
    d. 6.0×10^{23} g.

3. Summary of Key Concepts (continued)

14. The empirical formula for a compound containing 36 g carbon, 48 g oxygen, and 6 g hydrogen is
    a. $C_{36}H_6O_{48}$.
    b. CH_2O.
    c. C_6HO_8.
    d. $C_6H_{12}O_6$.

15. If substance A and substance B each have a mass of 16.0 g, then
    a. they must be the same substance.
    b. they each have the volume of 22.4 L at STP.
    c. each is 1 mol of substance.
    d. their weights are equal.

16. The equation for the synthesis of ammonia is $N_2 + 3 H_2 \rightarrow 2 NH_3$. How many moles of N_2 are needed to produce 6 mol NH_3?
    a. 3
    b. 6
    c. 1
    d. 2

17. If your expected yield for a reaction is 75 g, and your actual yield is 25 g, the percent yield is
    a. 25%.
    b. 33%.
    c. 50%.
    d. 75%.

4. States of Matter

Introduction and Key Concepts

After being filled partway to the top with hot water, a flexible, sealable plastic water bottle is placed upright and uncapped into a freezer. When the water has frozen solid, the bottle is removed from the freezer and immediately capped tightly. Later, after the ice has melted, the sides of the bottle seem as if they are being pressed together. Explain what has happened. Write your statements in the space below.

_____

_____

_____

You will need your response to help you review what you have learned by the end of Essential 4.

4.1 How do scientists explain gas behavior?

The following physical properties are common to all gases.
- Gases have mass.
- Gases are easily compressed.
- Gases fill their containers completely.
- Different gases can move through each other, or diffuse, rapidly.
- Gases exert pressure.
- A gas's pressure depends on its temperature.

The kinetic-molecular model, based on a description of the behavior of the particles making up a gas explains these properties. Rudolf Clausius, James Clerk Maxwell, and Ludwig Boltzmann were among the scientists who contributed ideas to the kinetic-molecular model.

The kinetic-molecular model makes the following assumptions:
- A gas is made up of small particles that have mass. The particles may be atoms or molecules.
- Relatively large distances separate the particles in a gas.
- The particles are in rapid, continuous, and random motion.
- Because the particles frequently collide with each other and with the walls of their container, they exert pressure. The pressure depends on the particles' velocity, which increases as the temperature rises.
- The particles' collisions are **elastic.** In an elastic collision, no energy of motion is lost.

4.2 How are gases measured?

Because the volume of a gas changes with pressure and temperature, the values of several variables must be known in order to describe a gas sample and predict its behavior. These interdependent variables are the amount of gas (n), volume (V), temperature (T), and pressure (P). The amount of gas is expressed in moles, volume is the volume of its container, and temperature is expressed in kelvins.

Air exerts atmospheric pressure on the Earth's surface. Atmospheric pressure varies with altitude, and is greatest at or below sea level, where it has the highest column of air above it. The weight of the air column is measured with a mercury **barometer,** an instrument that shows pressure as millimeters of mercury, atmospheres, or bars. The atmosphere presses down on a reservoir of mercury surrounding a mercury-containing glass tube, forcing the mercury to rise in the tube. The height of the mercury in the tube indicates how great the atmospheric pressure is. The unit of pressure is the pascal (Pa). One pascal is one newton of force per square

4. States of Matter (continued)

meter of area. One atmosphere (atm) equals 101.3 kilopascals (kPa), or 101,325 Pa; 760 mm Hg; or 14.7 lb/in². A standard atmosphere is close to the average atmospheric pressure at sea level.

The pressure of a gas in an enclosed container is measured with a **manometer.** In this instrument, the atmosphere and the enclosed gas press on the mercury at each end of a U-shaped tube. The height of the mercury in the tube is compared with its height when only the atmosphere is pressing on it.

A mole of any gas at standard temperature and pressure (STP) will occupy 22.4 L of volume. For easy comparison of different gases, properties of gases are always given for conditions of STP.

4.3 What are the gas laws?

The **kinetic-molecular theory** was refined by nineteenth-century chemists, but earlier chemists had worked out several laws describing the relationships among pressure, volume, and temperature.

The English chemist and physicist Robert Boyle (1627–1691) proposed a relationship that we call Boyle's law. His law shows that the volume of a gas sample decreases as its pressure increases. In other words, the pressure and volume of a sample of gas at constant temperature are inversely proportional to each other. Boyle's law is shown by the following equation.

$$PV = k_1$$

The value of k_1 depends on several things, and you do not need to know its actual value to use Boyle's law. Instead, you can compare the volume of a sample under different pressures, as PV always equals k_1.

$$P_1 V_1 = k_1 = P_2 V_2$$

When you know any three of the values, you can easily calculate the fourth.

Charles's law, proposed by Jacques Charles, shows the relationship between volume and temperature. According to this law, volume increases with temperature. In other words, the volume of a fixed amount of gas at constant pressure is directly proportional to its absolute temperature. Absolute temperature is given in kelvins, and equals its temperature in Celsius degrees plus 273. In theory, the lowest temperature possible is 0 K, or **absolute zero.** Charles's law is shown by the following equation.

$$V = k_2 T \quad \text{or} \quad \frac{V}{T} = k_2$$

This implies the following relationship between the volumes of the same sample under different temperatures.

$$\frac{V_1}{T_1} = k_2 = \frac{V_2}{T_2}$$

These laws are related to Avogadro's law, which states that equal volumes of gases at the same temperature and pressure contain an equal number of particles. Avogadro's law can be written

$$V = k_3 n.$$

Here, n = the number of moles. Recall that the volume of a mole of gas is called the **molar volume,** and that at STP (273 K and 1 atm), the molar volume is 22.4 L.

A fourth important law, formulated by the English chemist John Dalton (1766–1844), is Dalton's law of partial pressures. It states that the sum of the partial pressures (p) of all the components of a gas mixture is equal to the total pressure (P_T) of the mixture. Dalton's law of partial pressures is shown by the following equation.

$$P_T = p_a + p_b + p_c + \ldots$$

4.4 How does an ideal gas behave?

Combining Boyle's law, Charles's law, Avogadro's law, and Dalton's law, scientists have derived the ideal gas equation, which describes the physical behavior of an **ideal gas** in terms of

4. States of Matter (continued)

pressure, volume, temperature, and number of moles of gas. An ideal gas is a gas that is described by the kinetic-molecular theory, which assumes that the particles have no volume and exert no forces on each other. Because those assumptions do not apply to real gases, no ideal gas truly exists. However, the equation still can be used to describe real gases' behavior. The ideal gas equation is

$$PV = nRT$$

where R is a constant. As you can see, the equation combines parts of the above laws.

The value of R depends on the units used when the equation is set up in the form $R = PV/nT$. When they are given as atm-L/mol-K, $R = 0.0821$. When they are given as Pa-m³/ mol-K or J/ mol-K, $R = 8.314$. The temperature must be stated in kelvins (K).

The kinetic-molecular theory is theoretical, the ideal gas law empirical; that is, based on evidence. The model accounts for the law in three ways, assuming other factors remain constant.

- Gas pressure increases with the number of moles of gas.
- Gas pressure increases with increased temperature.
- Gas pressure increases with decreased volume of the gas's container.

When a model accounts for observations, that lends support to the model's accuracy. So far,

the kinetic-molecular theory has accounted for observations very well.

The gas laws have many applications. By adjusting different variables, you can make the gas in a balloon, for example, less dense—lighter per unit volume—than the surrounding air. Usually the practical way of making a balloon rise is to fill it with a gas, such as helium, that is already less dense than air. Or, a gas can be heated to inflate its container, increasing its volume and lowering its density.

When gases are mixed, gas particles move through each other by the process of **diffusion.** When the atoms or molecules diffuse through a hole so small that only one particle can go through at a time, the process is called **effusion.** Lighter gases effuse and diffuse more quickly than heavier gases do.

4.5 What are the condensed states of matter?

As you have seen, the kinetic-molecular theory accounts for the behavior of gases. However, it also helps explain other states of matter. Liquids and solids are referred to as condensed states of matter because substances have higher densities in those states than they have as gases.

A comparison of the physical properties of gases, liquids, and solids is shown below.

Comparison of Physical Properties of Gases, Liquids, and Solids

Physical Property	Gaseous state	Liquid state	Solid state
compressibility	high	slight	slight
density	low	high	high
volume	fills container	has definite volume	retains volume rigidly
shape	assumes shape of its container	assumes shape of its container	retains own shape
diffusion	rapid	slow	extremely slow, only at the surface
expansion on heating	high	low	low

4. States of Matter (continued)

The particles of a liquid are closer together than those of a gas, and those in a solid are very close and stay in a fixed arrangement. Because of the closeness of particles in condensed states, their density is greater than in gases, and compressibility is less.

According to the kinetic-molecular theory, a substance's state at room temperature depends on the strength of the attractions among its particles. The strongest attractive forces are in solids, those of moderate strength in liquids, and very weak attractive forces are in gases.

The energy of motion of molecules varies in different states, also. In solids, it is too low to overcome the forces among the particles. In liquids, it is great enough to allow the particles to separate and flow. In gases, the high energy makes it possible for the particles to escape from each other entirely, and to fill whatever container they are in.

Substances change state at characteristic temperatures. Water changes from a solid to a liquid at 0°C, and from a liquid to a gas at 100°C. All ionic compounds are solids at room temperature. Nearly all metals are solids at room temperature, also, because of their strong metallic bonds, which result from the attractive forces between positive ions and valence electrons. Substances that are liquids or gases at room temperature have covalent bonds.

Forces among different molecules are called **intermolecular forces;** those within the same molecules are called **intramolecular forces.** When a substance changes state, only the intermolecular forces must be overcome, as the molecules remain unchanged. Thus, a change in state is a physical, not a chemical, property.

The strength of the inter-molecular force among atoms increases for elements lower in the periodic table, along with increased atomic radius and mass. The strength of the attractive force is indicated by a substance's boiling point; the higher the boiling point is the greater the attractive force must be. At the boiling point, the particles can overcome the force, then separate and disperse.

Arrangement of Particles in Gases, Liquids, and Solids

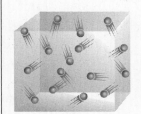  

gas
total disorder; particles have freedom of motion; particles far apart from one another

liquid
disorder; particles are free to move relative to one another; particles close together

crystalline solid
ordered arrangement; particles can vibrate, but remain in fixed positions; particles close together

---

4.6 What are the properties of liquids?

Liquids are characterized by physical properties of **viscosity** and **surface tension.** Viscosity is the "friction," or resistance to motion, that exists between the molecules when they move past each other. Surface tension is caused by the imbalance of attractive forces at the surface of a liquid that causes the surface to behave as if it had a film across it. These properties result from the intermolecular forces among the molecules.

Viscosity is the syrupy quality you see in honey or molasses. Viscosity increases at lower temperatures, when the particles making up the liquid have less energy of motion and cannot overcome the intermolecular forces attracting them to one another.

You may have seen an insect called a water strider walking across the surface of water

4. States of Matter (continued)

without sinking. This is possible because of the water's surface tension. The attractive forces among water molecules are so strong that it is as if the surface had a skin. Like viscosity, surface tension increases at lower temperatures.

Water, which makes up a large part of the Earth and its inhabitants, has unique properties that explain many phenomena.

- Water has a higher boiling point than most hydrogen compounds, and so it is liquid at room temperature.
- Water can absorb or release large quantities of heat without large changes in temperature. (It has an unusually high specific heat.)
- The solid form, ice, is less dense than liquid water. This is because the hydrogen bonding in ice is more extensive than in liquid water.
- Water has a high surface tension.
- The **heat of vaporization** for water is high. The heat of vaporization is the amount of heat required to change a given amount of a liquid to a gas (water vapor).
- Because of its polar molecular structure, water is an excellent **solvent.** A solvent is the substance that does the dissolving in a solution.

These properties result from the intermolecular force called hydrogen bonding, a strong force between a hydrogen atom on one molecule and the negative atom, such as oxygen, on another water molecule.

4.7 What are the properties of solids?

The particles in solids stay closely packed, unable to overcome the forces attracting them to one another. They can only vibrate in their fixed positions, like a person running in place. Most solids are crystalline in nature. A **crystalline solid** is made up of an organized, repeating pattern in three dimensions. The pattern is responsible for the shapes of large crystals and can be seen in small crystals by using a microscope.

The regular, repeating units in a crystal are called unit cells. Unit cells have definite geometric patterns that repeat themselves throughout the structure of the crystal. A compound always forms the same kind of unit cell, and thus the same kind of crystal. Sometimes the structure of a crystal includes water. Such solids are called hydrates. When they are heated and water is driven off, the crystals of the anhydrous compound look different from the hydrate.

Solids that are not crystalline are called **amorphous solids.** The word amorphous means shapeless. Amorphous solids are formed from cooling liquids, with the haphazard arrangement of molecules found in liquids.

The physical properties of solids—hardness, electrical conductivity, melting point, and so on—vary with the kind of particles making them up and with the strength of their intermolecular forces. Solids may be classed as metallic, molecular, ionic, and **covalent-network** on the basis of their properties. You have already read about the first three. Metallic solids are held together by metallic bonds; molecular, by hydrogen bonds and dipole attractions; and ionic, by electrostatic attractions. Covalent-network solids have strong covalent bonds that form a network extending throughout the crystal. They are very hard substances with high melting points, such as diamonds.

4.8 How does matter change from one state to another?

When a substance changes its state (or phase), it absorbs or releases energy and changes from one state—solid, liquid, or gas—to another. When a physical or chemical process gives off energy, it is called exothermic; when it absorbs energy, it is called endothermic.

The change of a liquid to a gas is called **vaporization,** or **evaporation.** The opposite change is **condensation.** Vaporization requires

4. States of Matter (continued)

the absorption of heat, as the molecules in the liquid must acquire enough energy of motion to increase their velocity and escape from the liquid's surface. A change in heat content is symbolized as ΔH, pronounced "delta H." The amount of heat needed, which depends on the substance, is called the **heat of vaporization.** To change from a gas to a liquid, the same substance must release the same amount of heat. When the rates of vaporization and condensation are equal, the number of molecules moving from one state to the other are equal, and equilibrium has been reached. At that time, the numbers of molecules in the gaseous state remain constant and exert a pressure called **equilibrium vapor pressure.** Vapor pressure varies with the substance and the temperature. When it is at least as high as atmospheric pressure, the boiling point has been reached. Similarly, freezing and melting require the release or absorption of heat. The amount

necessary to change a given amount of a solid to a liquid (ΔH) is its **heat of fusion.** The temperature at which solid and liquid states are in equilibrium is the **freezing point.**

Some solids can change directly to vapors without going through the liquid state. That change is called **sublimation** and the gas–solid conversion is called **deposition.**

Heating curves are graphs that show the temperature of a substance increasing as heat is added to it over time. At the freezing and boiling points, the curve forms plateaus while the substance absorbs the heat needed for melting or vaporization. The curves can also be read in the opposite direction, with the plateaus representing freezing or condensation.

Similar curves, called **phase diagrams,** show how both temperature and pressure determine a substance's state.

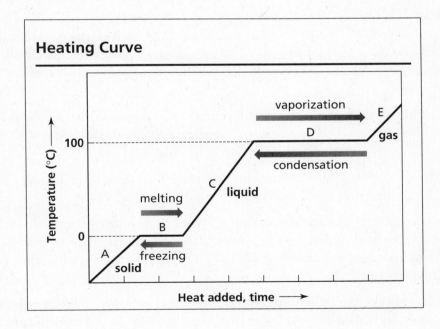

Heating Curve

4. Summary of Key Concepts

At the beginning of Essential 4, you were asked to explain why the sides of a sealable water bottle seemed to be pressed together after the ice in the bottle had thawed. Look at the statements that you wrote. In the space below, write how you would change your original statements before you review the key concepts.

_____

_____

_____

4.1 Gases have neither a definite shape nor definite volume. They are of low density and easily compressed. They exert pressure. The kinetic-molecular theory explains the observed behaviors of gases.

4.2 Air exerts pressure called atmospheric pressure. Gases are usually measured at standard temperature and pressure (STP). STP is defined as 0°C (273 K) and 1 atm.

4.3 Gas behaviors are determined by four variables: amount of gas (n), volume (V), temperature (T), and pressure (P). Boyle's law states that the pressure and volume of a gas at constant temperature are inversely proportional to each other. Charles's law states that the temperature and volume of a gas at constant pressure are directly proportional to each other. According to Avogadro's law, at constant temperature and pressure, equal volumes of different gases contain the same number of particles. The rule that the pressure of a mixture of gases is the sum of the component gases' partial pressures is Dalton's law.

4.4 The ideal gas equation, $PV = nRT$, mathematically relates the four gas variables. Though no ideal gas exists, the equation can be applied to real gases under most conditions. Density of a gas increases with molar mass and temperature. Lower-density gases diffuse and effuse faster than high-density gases.

4.5 A substance's physical state depends on its intermolecular forces; at room temperature, a substance with weak forces will be a gas; with moderate forces, a liquid; and with strong forces, a solid.

4.6 Liquids exhibit viscosity and surface tension. Because of hydrogen bonding among its molecules, water has unique properties.

4.7 In a crystalline solid, particles are arranged in an ordered, repeating pattern. In an amorphous solid, particles have the disordered arrangement that is characteristic of liquids. Forces among particles explain the properties of solids, which can be classified as metallic, molecular, ionic, and covalent-network.

4.8 Changes in state always require absorption or release of energy. Melting, vaporization, and sublimation are endothermic processes; freezing, condensation, and deposition are exothermic processes. Vapor in equilibrium with its liquid exerts vapor pressure, and the pressure increases with temperature. When vapor pressure is equal to the external atmospheric pressure, the liquid boils.

4. Summary of Key Concepts (continued)

Review Key Terms

On the line provided, write the term from the list that matches each description.

absolute zero	crystalline solid	kinetic-molecular theory
atmospheric pressure	deposition	manometer
Boyle's law	diffusion	STP
Charles's law	heating curve	surface tension
condensed state	intramolecular force	viscosity

_____ 1. liquid or solid state of matter

_____ 2. used for measuring gas pressure in a closed container

_____ 3. resistance to motion in a liquid

_____ 4. solid having repeating units arranged in a regular pattern

_____ 5. movement of gas particles

_____ 6. relates gas volume and temperature

_____ 7. 0 K

_____ 8. force exerted by air

_____ 9. holds a molecule together

_____ 10. theory that explains observed behaviors of gases

_____ 11. 273 K, 1 atm

_____ 12. filmlike surface that is the result of attractive forces

_____ 13. relates gas volume and pressure

_____ 14. reverse of sublimation

_____ 15. graph showing heat of absorption release during phase changes

4. Summary of Key Concepts (continued)

Assess Your Knowledge

Circle the letter of the answer that best completes the sentence.

1. According to the kinetic-molecular theory, gas particles do not
   a. stand still.
   b. speed up when the temperature increases.
   c. have mass.
   d. stay relatively far from each other.

2. The gas law that describes the relationship between volume and pressure is
   a. Avogadro's law.
   b. Charles's law.
   c. Boyle's law.
   d. Dalton's law.

3. Atmospheric pressure
   a. is always 760 mm Hg.
   b. is measured in kelvins.
   c. does not vary with humidity.
   d. varies with altitude.

4. If the pressure remains constant while the temperature is doubled, the volume of a sample of gas will
   a. be halved.
   b. increase by two times.
   c. increase by four times.
   d. stay the same.

5. Dalton's law describes
   a. the pressure of a sample of air.
   b. the temperature of a sample of air.
   c. the molar mass of a sample of air.
   d. none of the above.

6. Particles are attracted to each other by moderate forces, and slide past each other, in
   a. solids.
   b. gases.
   c. liquids.
   d. all states of matter.

4. Summary of Key Concepts (continued)

7. Surface tension
    a. decreases as the temperature falls.
    b. increases as the temperature rises.
    c. stays the same as the temperature falls.
    d. increases as the temperature falls.

8. An amorphous solid
    a. has unit cells arranged in regular patterns.
    b. has no regular pattern of particles.
    c. is very hard, with a high melting point.
    d. is formed from a superheated liquid.

9. Melting
    a. occurs at the same rate for every solid.
    b. increases as the temperature rises.
    c. is in equilibrium with freezing.
    d. is the same as sublimation.

10. The flat part of a heating curve indicates
    a. constant temperature.
    b. solid state.
    c. liquid state.
    d. gaseous state.

5. Chemical Equilibrium

Can you explain how the air around you, the saltwater in an aquarium, and the metal in coins are alike chemically? Using what you have learned in chemistry so far, briefly describe their major similarities and differences.

Introduction and Key Concepts

_____

_____

_____

You will need your response to help you review what you have learned by the end of Essential 5.

5.1 What is a solution?

You can see solutions all around you, including the air you breathe, the soda you drink, and the brass doorknobs in your home or school. Solutions are not always liquids; they may also be gases or solids.

When two or more substances are mixed homogeneously in a single physical state, the mixture is called a **solution.** One of the substances, called the **solvent,** dissolves the other, called the **solute.** More than one solute may be dissolved in the solution.

All solutions have the following properties:

• The particles are very small—atoms, molecules, or ions.

• The particles are mixed evenly at the molecular level.

• The particles do not separate if the solution stands under constant conditions.

A substance that will dissolve in another is said to be **soluble.** If one substance will not dissolve in another substance, it is said to be **insoluble.**

Solid solutions are mixtures of metals, such as copper and silver, or copper and gold. The most common type of metal solution is called an **alloy.** Different metals can be chosen to form an alloy with desirable characteristics for a specific purpose, such as for strength or a high melting point.

All mixtures of gases are considered solutions, because the gas molecules quickly mix with each other. Once mixed, they are not easily separated.

Liquid solutions may have gases, liquids, or solids dissolved in a liquid solvent. If two liquids can mix in any amount, they are said to be **miscible.** If they cannot mix in any proportion at all—oil and water, for example—they are said to be **immiscible.**

The most familiar liquid solvent is water. Solutions that contain water are called **aqueous** solutions. Some aqueous solutions conduct electricity, because the solute is ionic. When an ionic solute dissolves, its positive and negative ions separate from one another and can move freely. This makes it possible for an electric current to pass through the solution. A solute, such as table salt, NaCl, that dissolves in water to form an electricity-conducting solution is called an **electrolyte.** Substances that do not conduct electricity are called nonelectrolytes. Sugar is an example of an nonelectrolyte.

5.2 What are concentrated and dilute solutions?

A solution having a high proportion of solute is said to be **concentrated.** Thick maple syrup is an example of a concentrated solution. If you "water down" a concentrated solution, you are diluting it, or forming a **dilute solution.**

5. Chemical Equilibrium (continued)

The **concentration** of a solution is the amount of solute dissolved in the solvent. Concentration can be expressed in different ways, including **molarity, molality,** and **mole fraction.** As the names imply, they are all based on number of moles.

$$\text{molarity (M)} = \frac{\text{moles of solute}}{\text{liters of solution}}$$

$$\text{molality } (m) = \frac{\text{moles of solute}}{\text{kilogram of solvent}}$$

$$\text{mole fraction} = \frac{\text{moles of component (either solute or solvent)}}{\text{total moles of solution}}$$

Remember that you can find the number of moles of a substance if you know its mass and molar mass. Use as your conversion factor 1 mol divided by the mass in grams of 1 mol of the substance, and multiply by that conversion factor.

When a certain amount of solid solute is added to a solvent, there may be a point at which no more solute will dissolve. At that concentration, the solution is said to be **saturated** for those conditions of temperature and pressure. Before that saturation occurs, when there is less solute, the solution is said to be **unsaturated.** If you continue adding more solute to a saturated solution, it becomes **supersaturated.** Usually the solute will easily separate out from a supersaturated solution.

The amount of a solute that will dissolve in a certain solvent under given conditions is known as its **solubility.** Solubility is affected by the following factors.

• The nature of a specific solute and solvent— Polar solutes tend to dissolve in polar solvents, and nonpolar solutes in nonpolar solvents. This is called the "like dissolves like" rule.

• The temperature of the solute and solvent— Solubility of a gas in a liquid decreases with rising temperature, but in general the solubility of a solid in a liquid increases with rising temperature.
• The pressure of the solute and solvent— Pressure has little effect on the solubility of solids and liquids, but increases the solubility of gas in any solvent.

Solid solutes dissolve at different rates, and the rates are unrelated to their solubility. The rate at which a solute dissolves increases with the solute's surface area, with stirring, and with changes in temperature.

5.3 How are solutions formed?

When an ionic solution is placed in a solvent, a physical interaction begins. For example, if the solvent is water, the water molecules surround the solute. Wherever water molecules touch the solute surface, they separate (dissociate) the ions, which move into solution. Water molecules surround each positive or negative ion. This interaction between particles of solute and solvent is called **solvation.** If water is the solvent, solvation can also be called **hydration.**

Hydration of Sodium and Chloride Ions

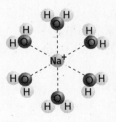

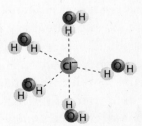

5. Chemical Equilibrium (continued)

During solvation, energy is used to break the bonds among solute particles and among solvent particles. These processes are endothermic. In contrast, energy is released when new attractions between solute and solvent particles are formed. The net result may be either endothermic or exothermic. If breaking attractions requires more energy than is released in forming attractions, heat will be absorbed in the overall process. If breaking attractions requires less energy than is released in forming attractions, heat will be given off in the overall process.

5.4 What are the collective effects of particles in solution?

While some properties of a solution depend on what the chemicals in the solution are, others result from the collective effect of the solute particles. Such a property is called a **colligative property.**

Four colligative properties are:

- **Vapor pressure reduction**—A solvent containing a nonvolatile solute has a lower vapor pressure than that of the pure solvent. The solvent particles take up space at the surface of the solution. This means that fewer solvent particles come into contact with the surface, and fewer leave the solution as vapor.
- **Boiling point elevation**—Because the vapor pressure is lower, a higher temperature is needed to raise the solution's vapor pressure up to atmospheric pressure (to reach the boiling point).
- **Freezing point depression**—This property also results from the lower vapor pressure. The freezing point of a substance is the temperature at which the vapor pressures of the solid and liquid phases are the same. The vapor pressure of the solution is reduced as the proportion of solute is increased. This lowers the temperature at which the solution and solid phase have the same vapor pressure, and so the freezing point is lower.

- **Osmotic pressure**—When two solutions of different concentrations are placed on opposite sides of a semipermeable membrane, molecules of the solvent will move from the less concentrated solution through the membrane to the more concentrated solution. The flow of molecules is called **osmosis,** and the pressure required to prevent is osmotic pressure.

5.5 How do processes reach a state of balance?

Chemical reactions do not always proceed from left to right. Some of them go in the opposite direction, as shown by the direction of the arrow in the equation for a reaction. If the equation has two arrows (or a double-headed arrow), the reaction can go in both directions. In a **reversible reaction,** the products can regenerate the original reactants. The equation for the reversible reaction between NO_2 and N_2O_4 is shown below.

$$2\ NO_2\ (g) \rightleftharpoons N_2O_4\ (g)$$

The reaction in which NO_2 forms N_2O_4 is called the forward reaction, and is indicated by the arrow that points to the right. The arrow pointing to the left indicates the reverse reaction, in which N_2O_4 forms NO_2. The two reactions are opposite processes. In the beginning, the forward rate is at its highest, and the reverse rate is 0. Over time, the forward rate decreases, and the reverse rate increases. When the rates of the forward and reverse reactions are equal, the overall reaction has reached **chemical equilibrium.** At that point, the concentrations of the products are constant because although the forward and reverse reactions will continue, the equal rates will maintain the concentrations the same.

5. Chemical Equilibrium (continued)

5.6 What is the law of chemical equilibrium?

At equilibrium, the concentrations of products and reactants in a reversible reaction can be shown in the form [X], where X stands for any product or reactant, and [] means "the concentration of." The reaction itself might be shown as

$$aA + bB \rightleftharpoons cC + dD$$

The lower-case letters are the coefficients of the equation, and the upper-case letters are the reactants and products. The equilibrium expression for this reaction is

$$\frac{[C]^c[D]^d}{[A]^a[B]^b} = K_{eq}, \text{ a constant}$$

The value of K_{eq} depends on the substances in the reaction. Every reversible reaction obeys this relationship and has a specific constant value for K_{eq}. If K_{eq} is about 1, the relative concentrations of reactants and products are the same at equilibrium. The larger K_{eq} is, the greater is the forward reaction rate compared with the reverse rate. The smaller the K_{eq}, the greater the reverse reaction rate. For example, in the reaction for the synthesis of ammonia

$$N_2 + 3H_2 \rightleftharpoons 2\,NH_3$$

At equilibrium,

$$K_{eq} = \frac{[NH_3]^2}{[N_2][H_2]^3}$$

At any point in a reaction, Q (the reaction quotient) can be calculated and compared with K_{eq}. At that point,

$$Q = \frac{[NH_3]^2}{[N_2][H_2]^3}$$

If $Q < K_{eq}$, there is too much of the reactant(s) present, and equilibrium has not been reached yet. If $Q > K_{eq}$, the reverse reaction will proceed until equilibrium is reached. If $Q = K_{eq}$, the reaction is at equilibrium.

5.7 How is equilibrium shifted?

In the 19th century, the French chemist Henri Le Chatelier (1850–1936) discovered an important principle about equilibrium. **Le Chatelier's principle** states that if a change in conditions is imposed on a system at equilibrium, the system will then shift in the forward or reverse direction to reduce the change. The changing conditions affect the concentrations of the reactants and products, and so studying the changed concentrations will help you see how the reaction will shift.

- *Changes in concentration.* If more of a reactant is added, or if some of a product is removed, the reaction will move in the direction that will restore the equilibrium concentration.
- *Changes in pressure.* In gaseous systems at equilibrium, increasing the pressure will increase the density of all the molecules in the system. The reaction will move in whichever direction produces fewer total molecules. For example, in the reaction

$$NH_4Cl(s) \rightleftharpoons NH_3(g) + HCl\,(g)$$

the reactant is a solid (*s*), and the products are gases (*g*). On the reactant side, there are 0 moles of gas and on the product side there are 2 moles of gas. If the pressure on the system is increased, the equilibrium of the reaction will shift to the left, decreasing the number of moles of gas in the system.

- *Changes in temperature.* If a reaction is exothermic, it can be shown as

$$A + B \rightleftharpoons C + heat$$

Increasing the temperature of the system will cause the reverse reaction to increase until equilibrium is reached.

The Haber process of synthesizing ammonia was a practical application of Le Chatelier's principle. The German chemist Fritz Haber (1868–1934) increased NH_3 production by removing the product and increasing pressure and temperature during the synthesis reaction.

5. Chemical Equilibrium (continued)

5.8 How do substances dissolve?

After the ions in an aqueous ionic solution dissociate and spread through the water, they may remain dissolved or they may attach themselves to the remaining solid. If they reform the original ionic compound, they precipitate as crystals.

When **dissolution,** or dissolving, and precipitation occur at equal rates, the ion concentrations in the solution are constant, and the whole system is said to have reached **solubility equilibrium.** A typical equation showing solubility equilibrium is

$$NaCl(s) \rightleftharpoons Na^+ (aq) + Cl^- (aq)$$

At equilibrium, a **solubility product** constant, K_{sp}, equals the product of the dissociated ions, or

$$K_{sp} = [Na^+] [Cl^-]$$

This equation is based on the solubility of an ionic salt in a solvent.

5.9 How do precipitates form?

A supersaturated solution is an unstable, nonequilibrium state achieved by manipulating the conditions of the solution, such as by raising its temperature. A precipitate will readily form in a supersaturated solution. The solubility product constant, K_{sp}, can be compared to the reaction quotient, Q, which in this case is called the **ion product,** to determine if an aqueous solution of ions is supersaturated and will form a precipitate. If $Q < K_{sp}$, then the solution is supersaturated, and a precipitate will form. At $Q = K_{sp}$, the solution is saturated, and if $Q < K_{sp}$, the solution is still unsaturated.

Sometimes a precipitate will form if two different aqueous solutions are mixed, as the result of a double-replacement reaction. For example,

$$AgNO_3(aq) + KBr(aq) \rightleftharpoons$$
$$AgBr(s) + KNO_3 (aq)$$

While some ions may join to form a compound that precipitates out, others may stay in solution as ions. Because these ions do not participate in the reaction, they are called spectator ions. The equation for the reaction can be shown as the complete ionic equation or, if shown without the spectator ions, the net ionic equation.

If more than one solute in a solution contains a given ion, the ion is called a common ion. Adding common ions can upset a system's equilibrium; the resulting **common-ion effect** lowers a substance's solubility in a solution containing the common ion. The common-ion effect is a shift in equilibrium that occurs because the concentration of an ion that is part of the equilibrium has changed. According to Le Chatelier's principle, if the concentration of a substance in a reaction is changed, the reaction will proceed in the direction that minimizes the change.

5. Summary of Key Concepts

At the beginning of Essential 5, you were asked to make statements comparing air, saltwater, and the metals in coins in chemical terms. Look at those statements again. Using what you have learned about solutions, add to or change your statements before you review the key concepts below.

_____

_____

_____

5.1 Solutions are homogeneous mixtures of two or more substances in a single physical state. A solution is made up of a solvent, which dissolves, and one or more solutes, which are dissolved. If a substance is soluble it will dissolve in another substance; an insoluble substance will not. An aqueous solution contains water as the solvent. Liquids that can mix with each other are said to be miscible. Immiscible liquids do not mix.

5.2 The concentration of a solution is the amount of solute in a given amount of solvent. It can be expressed as molarity, molality, and mole fraction. A saturated solution contains the maximum dissolved solute it can hold. If the solute is present in a lower amount, the solution is unsaturated; if the solution is forced to hold more solute than the maximum, it is supersaturated.

5.3 Solvation is a process in which solvent particles pull solute particles into solution and surround them. If water is the solvent, solvation is called hydration. Solubility of a solute is the extent to which it will dissolve in a solvent. It depends on the nature of the solute and solvent, the temperature, and the pressure of the solution.

5.4 Vapor pressure reduction, boiling point elevation, freezing point depression, and osmotic pressure are properties that depend on the concentration—and not the type—of the solute.

5.5 In a reversible reaction, the products can regenerate the original reactants. A reversible reaction reaches chemical equilibrium when the rates of the forward and reverse reactions are equal.

5.6 Every reaction at equilibrium has a specific equilibrium constant. The reaction quotient, Q, shows the ratio of product and reactant concentrations at any point and can be compared with K_{eq} to show in which direction the reaction will proceed.

5.7 Le Chatelier's principle states that a system disturbed from equilibrium will shift to regain equilibrium. Disturbances can include changes in concentrations, in pressure, or in temperature.

5.8 When an ionic solid is placed in water, the solid will dissolve. It may be reformed during the reverse process, precipitation. When dissolution and precipitation rates become equal, a state of equilibrium is reached, and the ion concentrations in solution are constant.

5.9 A precipitate will form if two aqueous solutions are mixed and a double-replacement reaction occurs. An ion contained in more than one solute in a solution is called a common ion. The presence of common ions in a solution can lower the solubility of an ionic solid added to the solution. This is called the common ion effect.

5. Summary of Key Concepts (continued)

Review Key Terms

On the line provided, write the term from the list that matches each description.

alloy   net ionic equation   spectator ion
Haber process   precipitation   supersaturated
hydration   reaction quotient   solvent
immiscible   reversible reaction   vapor pressure reduction
K_{eq} solute
molality   solution

_____ **1.** homogeneous mixture in a single physical state

_____ **2.** that which is dissolved

_____ **3.** dissolves another substance in a solution

_____ **4.** metals in solution

_____ **5.** will not mix in any proportions

_____ **6.** moles of solute per kilogram of solvent

_____ **7.** contains more than the maximum amount of solute

_____ **8.** solvation, with water as the solvent

_____ **9.** responsible for other colligative properties

_____ **10.** proceeds in the direction of either reactants or products

_____ **11.** constant showing relative concentrations at equilibrium

_____ **12.** shows relative concentrations of reactants or products at any point in reaction

_____ **13.** practical application of Le Chatelier's principle

_____ **14.** formation of an ionic compound that comes out of solution

_____ **15.** ion that does not participate in a reaction

_____ **16.** equation that does not include spectator ions

5. Summary of Key Concepts (continued)

Assess Your Knowledge

Circle the letter of the answer that best completes the sentence or answers the question.

1. Movement of water molecules through a semipermeable membrane is called
   a. diffusion.
   b. vapor pressure reduction.
   c. colligative.
   d. osmosis.

2. Which substance is an alloy?
   a. brass
   b. copper
   c. 24-karat gold
   d. salt water

3. What is the molarity of a solution containing 5.0 g H_2SO_4 in a 100-mL aqueous solution?
   a. 49.1 M
   b. 5.1 M
   c. 0.51 M
   d. 4.91 M

4. The rate at which a solute dissolves is not affected by
   a. temperature.
   b. stirring.
   c. identity of the solute.
   d. pressure of the solution.

5. In the reaction H_2 (g) + I_2 (g) $\rightleftharpoons$ 2 HI (g), the concentration of HI is
   a. [HI].
   b. [HI]^2.
   c. [2 HI].
   d. 2 [HI].

6. At equilibrium, Q
   a. $< K_{eq}$.
   b. $= 1$.
   c. $= K_{eq}$.
   d. $> K_{eq}$.

5. Summary of Key Concepts (continued)

7. In the reaction As_4O_6 (s) + 6 C (s) $\rightleftharpoons$ As_4 (g) + 6 CO (g), the formation of As_4 can be decreased by

   a. increasing the amount of C in the system.

   b. increasing the pressure on the system.

   c. removing CO as it is formed.

   d. removing As_4 as it is formed.

8. Before solubility equilibrium is attained, Q

   a. $> K_{sp}$.

   b. $> K_{eq}$.

   c. $= K_{sp}$.

   d. $< K_{sp}$.

9. For the reaction $Mg(OH)_2$ (s) $\rightleftharpoons$ Mg^{2+} (aq) + 2 OH^- (aq), K_{sp} =

   a. $[Mg^{2+}]^2[OH^-]^2$.

   b. $[Mg^{2+}]^2[OH^-]$.

   c. $[Mg^{2+}][OH^-]^2$.

   d. $[Mg^{2+}][OH^-]$.

10. When aqueous solutions of AgCl and $AgNO_3$ are mixed, the common ion is

    a. Ag^+.

    b. Cl^-.

    c. NO_3.

    d. none of the above.

6. Acids and Bases

Introduction and Key Concepts

When excess stomach acid rises into the lower esophagus, the acid causes a pain commonly called heartburn. Heartburn can often be relieved by taking an antacid tablet. How does the antacid tablet work? What happens to the excess stomach acid? Based on what you have learned so far in chemistry, write your statements in the space below.

_____

_____

_____

You will need your response to help you review what you have learned by the end of Essential 6.

6.1 What are acids and bases?

You can probably name some common acidic and basic substances already. Vinegar, lemon juice, and tomato juice contain acids, for example, while lye, baking soda, and soap contain bases. An acidic substance such as vinegar tastes sour and stings if it touches broken skin. Mild basic substances such as soap are bitter and feel slippery. What chemical properties account for these observations? Read on to find out the answer to this question.

The first successful definition of acids and bases was proposed by Svante Arrhenius in 1884. Arrhenius suggested that acids and bases could be understood in terms of the ions that they release when they dissolve in water. He proposed the following definitions:

- An **acid** is a substance that dissociates in water to produce hydrogen ions (H^+).
- A **base** is a substance that dissociates in water to produce hydroxide ions (OH^-).

The chemical formulas of acids that fit the Arrhenius definition are usually written with an H at the beginning. This emphasizes that they are sources of H^+ ions. Examples of Arrhenius acids are hydrochloric acid (HCl), sulfuric acid (H_2SO_4), and carbonic acid (H_2CO_3). In the same way, the formulas for Arrhenius bases include OH. Examples of Arrhenius bases are sodium hydroxide (NaOH), magnesium hydroxide ($Mg(OH)_2$), and calcium hydroxide ($Ca(OH)_2$).

Because it is dangerous to taste or touch an unknown substance, how can an acid or base be recognized? Acid-base **indicators** are substances that turn one color in an acidic solution and another color in a basic solution. Indicators are useful for determining whether a solution is acidic or basic. One of the most common acid-base indicators is litmus. An acid changes litmus paper from blue to red, and a base changes litmus from red to blue.

6.2 What happens when an acid and a base are mixed in solution?

If an acid and a base are mixed together, they react with each other. If the proper amounts of each are used, the reaction results in a solution that has none of the properties of an acid or base. In other words, the properties of both the acid and the base have been neutralized in the reaction. Such a reaction is called an acid-base **neutralization reaction.**

In a neutralization reaction, the H^+ ions from the acid combine with the OH^- ions of the base to form a molecule of HOH, commonly written H_2O, or water. Besides water, an acid-base neutralization reaction always produces a compound called a **salt.** Table salt, whose formula is NaCl, and NH_4NO_3 are two examples

6. Acids and Bases (continued)

of salts. A salt may be defined as an ionic compound formed from any cation (positive ion) other than H^+ and any anion (negative ion) other than OH^- or O^{2-}. In a neutralization reaction, the salt that is produced is formed from the cation of the base and the anion of the acid.

6.3 What are some of the properties of acids and bases?

Acids react vigorously with most metals, such as iron or aluminum, to produce hydrogen gas. This makes sense, because according to the Arrhenius definition an acid is a source of hydrogen ions. Unlike acids, bases do not react with most metals.

Another property of acids and bases is that they are electrolytes. An electrolyte is a substance that ionizes when it dissolves in water, and a solution that contains electrolytes conducts electricity. According to the Arrhenius definition, acids and bases release ions when they dissolve in water. Therefore, they are electolytes. When an acid or base is dissolved in water, the water conducts electricity quite well.

6.4 What are Brønsted-Lowry acids and bases?

Although the Arrhenius definition is useful, it has several limitations. One limitation is that the definition only applies to acids and bases that are dissolved in water. To overcome the limitations of the Arrhenius definition, a more general definition, called the Brønsted-Lowry definition, was proposed. According to the Brønsted-Lowry definition:

• An acid is any substance that can donate H^+ ions.

• A base is any substance that can accept H^+ ions.

What is an H^+ ion? It is a hydrogen atom that has lost one of its electrons. However, a hydrogen atom is the smallest possible atom, consisting of a nucleus of 1 proton surrounded by 1 electron. Therefore, an H^+ ion is actually just a proton. Another way to state the Brønsted-Lowry definition is that a Brønsted-Lowry acid is a proton donor, and a Brønsted-Lowry base is a proton acceptor.

Because H^+ ions are simply protons when they are dissolved in water they are strongly attracted to the electrons of surrounding water molecules. This interaction between water and protons forms an H_3O^+ ion, called a **hydronium ion.** The following equation shows the formation of hydronium ion.

$$H^+ + H_2O \rightarrow H_3O^+$$

From the Brønsted-Lowry perspective, a molecule of HCl transfers an H^+ ion to a water molecule to form hydronium ions (H_3O^+) and Cl^- ions. The HCl donates, or gives away, an H^+ ion, so it is the Brønsted-Lowry acid in this reaction. The water (H_2O) accepts the H^+ ion to form hydronium, so water is the Brønsted-Lowry base.

In other reactions, water can act as an acid by donating an H^+ ion. Any substance that can act as either an acid or base is called **amphoteric.** Because water can accept an H^+ ion in some reactions and donate one in others, water is amphoteric.

6. Acids and Bases (continued)

6.5 What are strong and weak acids and bases?

An acid such as HCl readily transfers H^+ ions to water, forming H_3O^+ and Cl^- ions. Therefore, HCl is called a strong acid. Strong acids react completely to form ions. In contrast, a weak acid does not readily transfer H^+ ions to water. The substances that most readily accept H^+ ions are called strong bases. Weak acids and bases react only partially with water. Many of the molecules of a weak acid or a weak base do not dissociate to form ions, and so the dissociation reaction reaches equilibrium rather than going to completion.

Sometimes an acid compound can become a base by losing an H^+ ion. Likewise, a base can become an acid in a reverse reaction by gaining an H^+ ion. When an acid loses an H^+ ion, it becomes this acid's **conjugate base.** When a base gains an H^+ ion, it becomes this base's **conjugate acid.** A pair of compounds that are identical except for an H^+ ion are a conjugate acid-base pair. Examples of such pairs are HCl and Cl^-, NH_3 and NH_4^+, and H_2O and OH^-. The stronger an acid, the weaker its conjugate base will be. The stronger the base, on the other hand, the weaker its conjugate acid.

6.6 How can the strengths of acids and bases be expressed with numbers?

When the products and reactants of a reaction reach equilibrium, the ratio of their concentrations always has the same value. This ratio is the equilibrium constant, or K_{eq}. For the reaction of any acid (symbolized by HA) with water, this constant is as follows.

$$K_{eq} = \frac{[H_3O^+][A^-]}{[HA][H_2O]}$$

For dilute solutions, the concentration of H_2O is essentially constant, and so chemists typically use a different expression, called the **acid dissociation constant,** or K_a. For any acid,

$$K_a = \frac{[H_3O^+][A^-]}{[HA]}$$

The greater an equilibrium constant, the further the reaction runs to completion. For acids, this means that the larger the K_a, the more the acid reacts with water to produce H_3O^+ ions. Therefore, the acid dissociation constant, K_a, is a measure of the strength of an acid. The greater the K_a, the stronger the acid.

In the same way, the **base dissociation constant,** or K_b, is derived from the equilibrium constant for a reaction with water. For any base, symbolized by B,

$$K_b = \frac{[HB^+][OH^-]}{[B]}$$

The stronger the base, the larger the concentration of hydroxide (OH^-) ions in the solution, and the larger the $[OH^-]$, the larger the K_b. Therefore, the base dissociation constant, K_b, is a measure of the strength of a base.

6. Acids and Bases (continued)

6.7 How are acids and bases recognized and named?

In a molecule of an acid, a hydrogen atom that can be donated is called an **acidic hydrogen.** Generally, an acidic hydrogen already has a slight positive charge and so is on the positive end of a polar covalent bond. Therefore, acidic hydrogens are usually bonded to very electronegative elements, such as oxygen, nitrogen, or members of the halogen family.

Chemists have identified thousands of acids. Most fall into the following three categories based on their composition and structure.

- **Binary acids** contain hydrogen and one other element (usually from Group 6A or 7A of the periodic table). An example is HCl.
- **Oxy acids** contain hydrogen, oxygen, and one other element. H_2SO_4 is an oxy acid.
- **Carboxylic acids** are organic acids, which means that they contain carbon atoms. Acetic acid ($HC_2H_3O_2$) is an example.

What makes a compound basic? A Brønsted-Lowry base always contains an unshared pair of electrons. With this unshared pair, the base attracts and bonds with an H^+ ion. Most Brønsted-Lowry bases fall into two categories: anions and amines.

- **Anions** are negatively charged ions. They have available electron pairs, and so they can function as bases (Cl^- is an example; its conjugate acid is HCl).
- **Amines** contain a nitrogen atom with an unshared pair of electrons, or an NH_2 group. Methylamine (CH_3NH_2) is an example of an amine.

Typically, the name of an acid comes from the name of the anion it produces when it dissociates. Here are three general rules to follow when naming an acid.

1. If the name of an anion ends in -ide, the name of the acid that produces it includes the name of the anion, a *hydro-* prefix, and an -*ic* ending. For example, HCl is *hydro*chloric acid.
2. If the name of an anion ends in -ate, the acid that produces it has an -*ic* ending but no prefix. Chloric acid, $HClO_3$, is an example.
3. If the name of an anion ends in -ite, the acid that produces it has an -*ous* ending but no prefix. An example is chlorous acid, $HClO_2$.

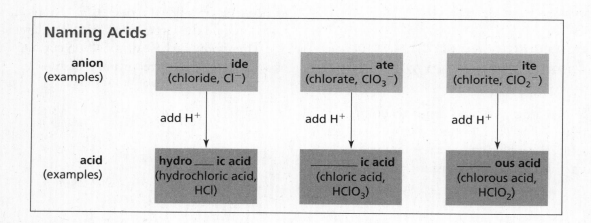

6. Acids and Bases *(continued)*

6.8 What is pH and where do acids and bases stand on the pH scale?

Acidity and basicity are measured on a scale that ranges from 0 to 14, called the pH scale. The most acidic substance possible has a pH of 0, and the most basic substance has a pH of 14. The center of the range is 7. This is the pH of pure water.

Because water is amphoteric—that is, it behaves both as an acid and a base—a water molecule can transfer an H^+ ion to another water molecule, forming an H_3O^+ ion and an OH^- ion. This reaction is called **self-ionization** of water. In pure water at 25°C, both H_3O^+ ions and OH^- ions are present, each at concentrations of 1.0×10^{-7} M. This fact can be expressed using a number called the **ion-product constant** for water, K_w, where

$$K_w = [H_3O^+][OH^-]$$
$$= (1.0 \times 10^{-7})(1.0 \times 10^{-7})$$
$$= 1.0 \times 10^{-14}$$

In all solutions at 25°C, the product of the concentrations of H_3O^+ and OH^- ions equals 1.0×10^{-14}. If the concentration of H_3O^+ ions in a solution is greater than 1.0×10^{-7} M, the solution is acidic. If the concentration of OH^- ions is greater than 1.0×10^{-7} M, the solution is basic. The solution is neutral if the concentrations of both ions equal 1.0×10^{-7} M.

For most solutions, the molar concentration of H_3O^+ ions is a very small number. To make handling such small numbers more convenient, the pH scale is based on logarithms. The pH of a solution is −1 times the base 10 logarithm of the H_3O^+ concentration: $pH = -\log[H_3O^+]$. The

exponent of 10 in the number 1.0×10^{-7} is −7. Therefore, the pH of pure water is 7. The smaller the pH, the more acidic the solution. Solutions with a pH less than 7 are acids, and solutions with a pH greater than 7 are bases.

Ion Concentration and pH

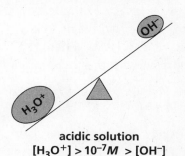

acidic solution
$[H_3O^+] > 10^{-7}M > [OH^-]$

neutral solution
$[H_3O^+] = [OH^-] = 10^{-7}M$

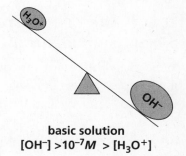

basic solution
$[OH^-] > 10^{-7}M > [H_3O^+]$

The ion that is more concentrated than $10^{-7}M$ determines the acidity or basicity of the solution.

6. Acids and Bases (continued)

6.9 What do buffers do?

A **buffer** is a mixture, typically of acids and bases, that keeps a solution's pH constant by releasing or absorbing H^+ ions. Buffers play an important role in living things by helping to control the pH within narrow limits.

Often buffers are made from a weak acid and its conjugate base. For example, a buffer can be made from acetic acid ($HC_2H_3O_2$) and the acetate ion ($C_2H_3O_2^-$). When H_3O^+ ions are added, they react with the acetate ion, as follows:

$$H_3O^+ (aq) + C_2H_3O_2^- (aq) \rightarrow$$
$$H_2O (l) + HC_2H_3O_2 (aq)$$

When OH^- ions are added to the solution, they react with the acetic acid component:

$$OH^- (aq) + HC_2H_3O_2 (aq) \rightarrow$$
$$H_2O (l) + C_2H_3O_2^- (aq)$$

Whichever ion is added, the buffer solution reacts with it to restore the original pH. The amount of acid or base that a buffer can neutralize is called its buffer capacity.

6.10 How is the concentration of an acid or base measured?

The most convenient way to quantify the amount of an acid or a base in a solution is with a procedure called an acid-base titration. An acid-base titration is a carefully controlled neutralization reaction. To run a titration on a solution of unknown concentration of an acid or a base, a second solution, called a standard solution, is also needed. A standard solution contains an acid or a base in a known concentration.

During the titration procedure, the standard solution is slowly added to the unknown solution. As the two solutions mix, the acid in one solution neutralizes the base in the other. Eventually, enough standard solution is added to neutralize all the acid or base in the unknown solution. The point at which this occurs is called the equivalence point.

Before beginning the titration, an indicator is added to the unknown solution. During the titration, the concentration at which the indicator changes color is called the end point of the titration. If the indicator is chosen correctly, the end point will be very close to the equivalence point.

Chemists carefully monitor how the pH changes throughout the titration. These pH data are typically presented in a graph, called a titration curve. If the unknown solution contains a combination of a strong and a weak acid and base, the titration curve rises or falls sharply near the equivalence point of the solution.

6. Summary of Key Concepts

At the beginning of Essential 6, you were asked if you could make any statements about how antacid tablets work to relieve heartburn. Look again at those statements. In the space below, add to or change your original statements based on what you have learned in Essential 6. Then review the key concepts below.

_____

_____

_____

6.1 Acids taste sour, react with metals to produce hydrogen, and turn litmus paper red. Bases taste bitter, are slippery, and turn litmus paper blue. An acid is a substance that dissociates in water to produce hydrogen ions (H^+). A base dissociates in water to produce hydroxide ions (OH^-).

6.2 When acids and bases react with each other, they neutralize each other's characteristic properties, producing H_2O and a salt. A neutralization reaction is a reaction in which acids and bases lose their characteristics.

6.3 Acids react vigorously with metals to produce hydrogen gas, although bases do not. Acids and bases are electrolytes because they dissociate to form ions in water.

6.4 According to the Brønsted-Lowry definition, an acid is a proton donor and a base is a proton acceptor. A hydronium ion, H_3O^+, is formed when water molecules accept a third proton, H^+, from the solution. Amphoteric substances, such as water, act as both acids and bases.

6.5 A strong acid or base completely ionizes in water. Acids and bases are present as conjugate pairs in a solution. A strong acid has a weak conjugate base, and a strong base has a weak conjugate acid.

6.6 The strength of acids or bases is shown by the acid dissociation constant (K_a) or base dissociation constant (K_b), which reflect the relative concentrations of OH^- and H^+ ions.

6.7 An acidic hydrogen is a hydrogen atom that can be donated. Acids are categorized as binary, oxy, or carboxylic. Bases are anions or amines. The names of acids and bases are formed according to three general rules.

6.8 The measure of acidity or basicity is expressed using the pH scale. The pH of a solution is -1 times the base 10 logarithm of the H_3O^+ concentration: $pH = -\log[H_3O^+]$. If the pH of a solution is less than 7, it is acidic; if greater than 7, it is basic.

6.9 A buffer is a mixture of chemicals (usually a conjugate pair of a weak acid and its base) that react with H_3O^+ or OH^- ions to maintain the pH of a solution.

6.10 Acid-base titrations are used to calculate the concentration of acid or base in a solution by carrying out a neutralization reaction with a standard solution whose concentration is known. The equivalence point of a titration is reached when the standard solution has neutralized the unknown solution. At this point, the number of moles of H^+ ions from the acid equals the number of moles of OH^- ions from the base.

6. Summary of Key Concepts (continued)

Review Key Terms

On the line provided, write the term from the list that matches each description.

acid
amphoteric
base
buffer
dissociation constant
hydronium ion
neutralization reaction
pH
salt
titration end point

_____ 1. results in formation of salt and water

_____ 2. indicates strength of acid or base

_____ 3. can act as acid or base

_____ 4. formed from water and H^+ ion

_____ 5. accepts H^+ ions

_____ 6. ionic compound formed from neutralization reaction

_____ 7. numerical indication of hydronium ion concentration

_____ 8. proton donor

_____ 9. maintains pH of a solution

_____ 10. change in indicator color shows reaction is over

6. Summary of Key Concepts (continued)

Assess Your Knowledge

Circle the letter of the answer that best completes the sentence or answers the question.

1. A base
   a. tastes sour.
   b. reacts with metals to produce hydrogen gas.
   c. feels slippery.
   d. is a proton donor.

2. In a water solution, a weak base
   a. is completely ionized.
   b. is partially ionized.
   c. releases H^+ ions.
   d. is not ionized.

3. The K_a of a strong acid
   a. is greater than the K_a of a weak acid.
   b. equals the K_a of a strong base.
   c. equals the K_b of its conjugate base.
   d. is less than 1.

4. In water, a weak acid and strong base will produce
   a. pure water.
   b. a neutral salt solution.
   c. an acidic salt solution.
   d. a basic salt solution.

5. HCl, hydrochloric acid, is a(n)
   a. carboxylic acid.
   b. binary acid.
   c. oxy acid.
   d. weak acid.

6. In pure water at 25°C, $[H_3O^+]$ equals
   a. 7 M.
   b. 1.0×10^{-14} M.
   c. 1.0×10^{-7} M.
   d. 0 M.

6. *Summary of Key Concepts* (continued)

7. A pH of 8 indicates a
   a. basic solution.
   b. neutral solution.
   c. very acidic solution.
   d. slightly acidic solution.

8. Which substances might be used to make a buffer solution?
   a. strong acid and its conjugate base
   b. weak acid and its conjugate base
   c. strong acid and a weak acid
   d. strong base and a weak base

9. A standard solution is used as a titration
   a. solution with known concentration.
   b. solution with unknown concentration.
   c. indicator.
   d. base solution.

10. Litmus is an example of a(n)
    a. buffer.
    b. acid.
    c. indicator.
    d. base.

7. Redox Chemistry

Introduction and Key Concepts

To prevent silver objects from tarnishing during storage, some people wrap the objects tightly in aluminum foil. Using terms you have learned so far in chemistry, explain why you think this might be effective. Write your statements in the space below.

_____

_____

_____

You will need your response to help you review what you have learned by the end of the lesson.

7.1 What is a redox reaction?

Although you might think the word *redox* sounds like the brand name of a detergent, it is simply a short way of saying "reduction and oxidation." Originally, oxidation was used to describe reactions in which oxygen was added to a reactant, and reduction at first meant the removal of oxygen from a compound. Oxygen is very electronegative and tends to gain electrons when it reacts with other substances. For example, when magnesium reacts with oxygen it changes from Mg to Mg^{2+}; in other words, a magnesium atom loses 2 electrons. Studying oxidation reactions reveals that substances lose electrons when they are oxidized. On the other hand, substances gain electrons when they are reduced.

Chemists today use the terms oxidation and reduction in a broader way to include reactions that do not involve oxygen. Oxidation and reduction are now defined in terms of the movements of electrons.

- **Oxidation** is the process by which a substance *loses* one or more electrons.
- **Reduction** is the process by which a substance *gains* one or more electrons.

You may find it helpful to use the expression OIL RIG to remember these definitions: OIL = Oxidation Is Loss of electrons; RIG = Reduction Is Gain of electrons.

Oxidation and reduction always occur together. Because matter cannot simply disappear, when electrons are lost by one substance in a reaction, they are gained by another substance. Because the processes of oxidation and reduction always occur together, reactions in which electrons are transferred between reactants are called **oxidation-reduction reactions,** or simply **redox reactions.**

7.2 How can we keep track of changes in oxidation in a redox reaction?

In balancing redox reactions, and in identifying which substances are oxidized or reduced, it is often useful to know the **oxidation number** of each atom. This number tells what charge an atom would have in a compound if all the electrons in each bond belonged to the more electronegative atom in the bond instead of being shared. For example, in the compound CH_4, the oxidation number of C is -4, and each H has an oxidation number of $+1$. Be careful not to confuse oxidation numbers with ionic charges. Notice that oxidation numbers are preceded by the charge sign (for example, $+1$), and ionic charges are followed by the charge sign ($1+$).

Although oxidation numbers can be determined by studying the bonding in a

7. Redox Chemistry (continued)

substance, it is easier to find them by using the following rules:

1. The oxidation number of an atom in an uncombined element is 0.

Example:

Atoms in O_2 have an oxidation number of 0.

2. The oxidation number for atoms in monatomic ions is the same as the charge on the ion.

Examples:

H^+ has an oxidation number of $+1$.
Ca^{2+} has an oxidation number of -2.

3. In compounds, the oxidation number of each atom usually corresponds to the element's column in the periodic table.

   a. Group 1A elements are always $+1$.
   b. Group 2A elements are always $+2$.
   c. Aluminum (Al) is always $+3$.
   d. Fluorine (F) is always -1.
   e. Hydrogen (H) is $+1$ when combined with nonmetals.
   f. Oxygen (O) is -2 in most compounds.

4. After adding, subtracting, and multiplying the individual oxidation numbers of all the atoms in the formula for a compound, the result must be 0.

Example:

In $K_2Cr_2O_7$, the oxidation number of K is $+1$ and of O is -2. What is the oxidation number of Cr_2?

First, $[2 \times (+1)] + [7 \times (-2)] =$
$2 - 14 = -12$

For the total oxidation number of the compound to equal 0, the Cr_2 must have an oxidation number of 12.

Therefore, the oxidation number of each Cr must be $+6$.

5. After adding, subtracting, and multiplying the individual oxidation numbers of all the atoms in the formula for a polyatomic ion, the result must equal the charge of the ion.

Examples:

In MnO_2, the Mn has an oxidation number of $+4$, because $[+4 - [2 \times (-2)] = 0$.
In MnO_4^-, the Mn is $+7$, because $+7 - [4 \times (-2)] = -1$, which is the same as the ionic charge of $1-$.
In MnO_4^{2-}, the Mn is $+6$, because $+6 - [4 \times (-2)] = -2$, the ionic charge.

In any redox reaction, at least one atom increases in oxidation number while another atom decreases in oxidation number. In oxidation, an atom loses an electron, becomes more positive,

Summary of Relationships Between Redox Reactions and Oxidation Number	
Oxidation	**Reduction**
loss of electrons	gain of electrons
increase in oxidation number	decrease in oxidation number

and its oxidation number increases. In reduction, an atom gains an electron, becomes more negative, and its oxidation number decreases. The following table summarizes those relationships.

7.3 What is the difference between an oxidizing agent and a reducing agent?

The terms oxidation and reduction refer to the processes of losing or gaining electrons. When chemists say that one substance oxidizes another, they mean that the first substance causes the second to lose one or more electrons. Likewise, when they say that one substance reduces another, they mean that the first substance causes the second to gain electrons.

An **oxidizing agent** causes the oxidation of another substance by accepting electrons from that substance. However, because the oxidizing agent gains the electrons that the other substance has lost, the oxidizing agent is itself reduced as a result of the reaction. Similarly, a

7. Redox Chemistry *(continued)*

reducing agent causes reduction by providing electrons to another substance. Because the reducing agent ends up with fewer electrons as a result of the reaction, the reducing agent has itself been oxidized.

Whether you choose to think of the redox reaction in terms of the substance that is doing the oxidizing (or reducing) or in terms of the substance that is being reduced (or oxidized) depends on which reactant you are most interested in.

7.4 What kinds of redox reactions are there?

There are three general types of redox reactions: direct combination (or synthesis), decomposition, and single-replacement.

In direct combination reactions, two or more elements on the left side of the equation join to form a single compound on the right side. The oxidation numbers for all elements on the left side of the equation in direct combination reactions are 0.

Decomposition reactions are the opposite of direct combination reactions. A compound on the left side of the equation breaks down to form free elements on the right side. The oxidation numbers are 0 for the free elements.

In a single-replacement reaction, a free element becomes an ion, and another ion becomes a free element. For that to occur, the oxidation number of each must change.

A common and important type of single-replacement reaction is the replacement of one metal by another. For example, when copper metal is placed in a solution with silver nitrate, copper nitrate is produced along with metallic silver.

$$Cu\ (s) + 2\ AgNO_3\ (aq) \rightarrow$$
$$Cu(NO_3)_2\ (aq) + 2\ Ag\ (s)$$

In this reaction, the copper (Cu) atoms lose electrons and become Cu^{2+} ions, while the silver

(Ag) is reduced. The copper ions then join with nitrate to form copper nitrate.

To predict whether a given metal will react with and replace another, chemists refer to an activity series of metals. In an activity series, metals are listed in order of their reactivity, with the most reactive ones at the top of the list. A metal can replace only those metals below it in the activity series. At the top of the list are metals that are so reactive that they can replace hydrogen from water, as illustrated in the following reaction between sodium and water:

$$2\ Na\ (s) + 2\ H_2O\ (l) \rightarrow 2\ NaOH\ (aq) + H_2\ (g)$$

The activity series ranks metals by their ease of oxidation. A metal that is easily oxidized becomes an ion that is not easily reduced. The metals at the bottom of the list are very resistant to oxidation.

7.5 How are redox reactions useful?

Redox reactions are important in many areas of industry and technology, and are a necessary part of many household items that make life more interesting and convenient. Here are a few examples of their uses:

- *Bleaching.* Color is the result of the movement of electrons between different quantum energy levels of the atoms of the material. Those electrons can be removed by bleaches, which are oxidizing agents.
- *Fuels.* Oxidation of fuels releases heat that can be used to do useful work.
- *Photography.* The processing of images is based on redox reactions of silver halides.
- *Preventing corrosion.* Corrosion is a redox reaction that can be prevented by coating the surface of the metal to keep oxygen, water, and other oxidizing substances from coming into direct contact with the metal. Corrosion can also be prevented by coating the metal with another metal that is more readily oxidized (in other words, that is listed higher in the activity series).

7. Redox Chemistry (continued)

7.6 How are equations for redox reactions balanced?

Chemists and chemical engineers use balanced equations to predict and control what happens in a redox reaction. The most important principle to keep in mind when balancing redox equations is that the number of electrons lost in an oxidation process (increase in oxidation number) must equal the number of electrons gained in the reduction process (decrease in oxidation number). To balance a redox equation, no matter how complicated it might look, follow these steps:

1. Write the equation and above each element in the equation write the oxidation number for that element. Be sure to write the oxidation number for each atom, even when more than one atom is present in a compound.

$$\overset{0}{S}\ (s) + \overset{+1\ +5\ -2}{HNO_3}\ (aq) \rightarrow$$
$$\overset{+4\ -2}{SO_2}\ (g) + \overset{+2\ -2}{NO}\ (g) + \overset{+1\ -2}{H_2O}\ (l)$$

2. Identify which element is oxidized and which is reduced, then determine the change in oxidation number of each element.

3. Use a bracket to connect each element on the left side of the equation with the same element on the right side. On top of each bracket, write the change in oxidation number for that element.

$$\overset{0}{S}\ (s) + \overset{+1\ +5\ -2}{HNO_3}\ (aq) \rightarrow \overset{+4\ -2}{SO_2}\ (g) + \overset{+2\ -2}{NO}\ (g) + \overset{+1\ -2}{H_2O}\ (l)$$

(bracket labeled +4 from S to SO₂; bracket labeled −3 from HNO₃ to NO)

4. Choose the coefficients that make the total increase in oxidation number equal the total decrease in oxidation number.

$$\overset{0}{3\ S}\ (s) + \overset{+1\ +5\ -2}{4\ HNO_3}\ (aq) \rightarrow \overset{+4\ -2}{SO_2}\ (g)$$
$$+ \overset{+2\ -2}{NO}\ (g) + \overset{+1\ -2}{H_2O}\ (l)$$

(bracket labeled 3(+4) = +12; bracket labeled 4(−3) = −12)

5. Look at how many atoms there are of each of the other elements and write coefficients so that both sides of the equation have the same number of each atom. Leave any H and O atoms for last.

$$\overset{0}{3\ S}\ (s) + \overset{+1\ +5\ -2}{4\ HNO_3}\ (aq) \rightarrow \overset{+4\ -2}{3\ SO_2}\ (g)$$
$$+ \overset{+2\ -2}{4\ NO}\ (g) + \overset{+1\ -2}{2\ H_2O}\ (l)$$

(bracket labeled 3(+4) = +12; bracket labeled 4(−3) = −12)

7.7 How can redox reactions be used to generate electricity?

Devices that use redox reactions either to produce or to use electricity are called electrochemical cells. Electrochemical cells that produce electricity as the result of redox reactions are called **voltaic cells.** A battery consists of one or more voltaic cells.

The sites where oxidation and reduction take place in electrochemical cells are called electrodes. Electrodes are electrical conductors made of metals or graphite. They carry electricity into or out of the cell. The electrode at which oxidation occurs is called the **anode,** which has a negative charge, and the electrode at which reduction occurs is the **cathode,** which has a positive charge.

7. Redox Chemistry (continued)

The spontaneous redox reaction between zinc metal and a solution of copper sulfate is one reaction that can be used to make a voltaic cell. In this reaction, zinc metal is oxidized and copper ions are reduced.

$$Zn\ (s) + Cu\ SO_4\ (aq) \rightarrow Zn\ SO_4\ (aq) + Cu\ (s)$$

The oxidation portion of the reaction is

$$Zn\ (s) \rightarrow Zn^{2+}\ (aq) + 2e^-$$

where $2e^-$ represents the two electrons that are released for each atom of zinc. The reduction portion of the reaction is

$$Cu^{2+}\ (aq) + 2e^- \rightarrow Cu\ (s)$$

showing that each Cu^{2+} ion accepts two electrons.

If a strip of zinc is placed in a beaker with copper ions, electrons transfer directly between Zn atoms and Cu^{2+} ions. However, if a strip of zinc is placed in a solution of zinc sulfate in one beaker, and a copper strip is placed in a copper sulfate solution in a separate beaker, then the strip of zinc metal can serve as an anode in the first solution and the strip of copper can serve as the cathode in the second. Each beaker serves as a voltaic **half-cell** in which the oxidation and reduction portions of the redox reaction take place separately. A wire connects the zinc anode to the copper cathode. Electric current will flow between the zinc anode and the copper cathode, as the zinc releases electrons to become Zn^{2+}.

For the current to continue flowing, however, ions must somehow be transferred from one cell to the other to keep the number of positive and negative ions equal in both beakers. Otherwise, electric charge will accumulate in each beaker instead of flowing between them. One way to transfer ions is by using a tube filled with electrolyte solution, called a salt bridge.

7.8 How can the strengths of redox reactions be measured and compared?

The ability of a reaction in a voltaic cell to move electrons through a wire from one electrode to another is called the electrical potential of the cell, or **cell potential.** The word *potential* refers to the ability to do work. The cell potential represents the difference in the electrical potential energy between the two electrodes of the cell. Cell potential is measured in units called volts (V), named for the Italian scientist Alessandro Volta, who built the first battery in 1800. The voltage of a cell represents the force with which each electron is "pushed" as it moves from one electrode to the other. That force can be used to do work, such as powering an electric motor. The role of voltage may be compared to water pressure in pipes.

The voltage, or cell potential, for each redox reaction is different. For example, the voltage of the zinc-copper cell discussed in section 7.7 is about 1 volt. The cell potential depends on the potential, or strength, of the oxidation reaction at the anode, and the potential of the reduction reaction at the cathode. Adding the oxidation potential ("electron pushing") to the reduction potential ("electron pulling") gives the total potential for the cell as shown in the following equation.

$$E_{cell} = E_{oxidation} + E_{reduction}$$

The exact voltage associated with a redox reaction depends on the temperature, pressure, and the concentrations of ions. By agreeing to make the standard conditions for comparing redox reactions 298 K at 101.3 kPa in 1 M water, chemists can use voltage as a way to compare the

7. Redox Chemistry (continued)

oxidation and reduction potentials of various redox reactions. Chemists have chosen to use the reduction reaction at standard conditions of H^+ ions to form H_2 as their yardstick. This reaction is assigned a standard reduction potential of exactly zero, and the voltages of all other reduction reactions are compared to the voltages of this one to show their standard reduction potentials. The more positive the standard reduction potential of a molecule or ion, the more easily that molecule or ion is reduced. The more negative the standard reduction potential, the harder the molecule or ion is to reduce.

The standard oxidation potential of a molecule or ion has the same magnitude or size as its standard reduction potential, but the standard oxidation potential is opposite in sign. Therefore, the more positive the standard oxidation potential of a molecule or ion, the more easily that molecule or ion is oxidized.

7.9 What types of batteries are there?

Batteries are voltaic cells in which spontaneous redox reactions are used to generate an electric current. The oxidizing and reducing agents are eventually used up in a battery, and the battery loses its effectiveness. Rechargeable batteries use an outside power source to reverse the reactions at the electrodes and restore the battery's effectiveness. Nonrechargeable batteries are based on redox reactions that cannot be reversed. The following are a few types of batteries in common use.

• The common dry cell consists of a zinc container filed with a paste mixture of zinc chloride ($ZnCl_2$), manganese(IV) oxide (MnO_2), ammonium chloride (NH_4Cl), and water. The zinc is oxidized in the battery, and MnO_2 is reduced, to produce a flow of electrons. Common dry cells (flashlight batteries) are relatively cheap to manufacture, but they have several disadvantages. They are nonrechargeable, the zinc reacts with the acidic ammonium ions, causing the cell to run down, and the voltage dips whenever current is drawn quickly from the cell.

• In the alkaline dry cell, KOH is used instead of the NH_4Cl electrolyte that is used in common dry cells. Because alkaline KOH does not react with zinc as readily as acidic NH_4Cl, alkaline dry cells have a longer shelf life than do common dry cells. However, because alkaline dry cells have a more elaborate design, they are more expensive. Alkaline dry cells are used in devices such as calculators.

• The electrodes of the lead storage battery, or car battery, are made of alternating sheets of lead and lead dioxide, with sulfuric acid being used as the electrolyte. Lead is oxidized and therefore serves as the anode, and lead dioxide is reduced at the cathode. Both the oxidation and the reduction reactions produce lead(II) sulfate ($PbSO_4$). The lead sulfate is insoluble, making it possible to reverse the redox reactions by applying an electric current.

• Nickel-cadmium batteries are also rechargeable. The anode in this type of battery is made of cadmium. Cadmium is oxidized to form Cd^{2+}, which then reacts with OH^- ions to form $Cd(OH)_2$. At the cathode, NiO_2 is reduced to become $Ni(OH)_2$. These batteries are used in cordless appliances.

• Fuel cells are voltaic cells that are continuously supplied with fuel from an external reservoir, so that they do not run down like ordinary batteries. They are highly efficient (about 90 percent) at converting chemical energy into electricity. A hydrogen-oxygen fuel cell supplies the space shuttle with electric power. A stream of hydrogen flows into the anode compartment of the cell where it is oxidized, while a stream of oxygen is reduced in the cathode compartment. The overall reaction is simply the oxidation of H_2 to produce water— which the astronauts then use for drinking.

7. Redox Chemistry (continued)

7.10 How do we use electrolysis?

The redox reactions used in batteries are spontaneous reactions. They do not require outside energy in order to proceed; in fact, they serve as energy sources. The process by which an outside source of electricity is used to drive a nonspontaneous redox reaction is called **electrolysis.** As in a battery, electrons in electrolysis flow from the anode, which is the site of oxidation, to the cathode, which is the site of reduction. However, because the redox reactions in electrolysis do not occur spontaneously, an outside source of electricity is needed to "push" the electrons from the anode to the cathode.

Electrolysis has practical uses in industry. The following are examples.

- Electrolysis can decompose molten sodium chloride to provide a commercial source of the elements sodium and chlorine. In this process, sodium ions are reduced and chloride ions are oxidized.

- When electrodes connected to a power supply are placed in water, the water is can be electrolyzed, forming H_2 at the anode and O_2 at the cathode.
- If aqueous sodium chloride is electrolyzed, chlorine gas and hydrogen gas are produced.
- Electrolysis is used to deposit a thin coating of protective metal on an object in a process called **electroplating.** The object to be electroplated, such as a spoon, for example, serves as the cathode, while the electroplating metal serves as the anode. The metal is first oxidized. Then it migrates through the electrolytic solution to the cathode, which is object to be electroplated, where the metal is reduced and becomes attached to the object.

7. Summary of Key Concepts

At the beginning of Essential 7, you were asked to make statements about why wrapping silver in aluminum foil helps keep the silver from tarnishing. Look at those statements again. Using what you have learned in Essential 7, add to or change your statements before you review the key concepts below.

_____

_____

_____

7.1 When a substance loses electrons in a reaction, it is oxidized. If a substance gains electrons, it is reduced. Oxidation and reduction reductions always occur together, and are called redox reactions.

7.2 An atom's oxidation number is the charge it would have if the electrons in each bond were transferred completely to the more electronegative atom. Finding oxidation numbers of each atom in a reaction can help in understanding what takes place during the reaction.

7.3 A redox reaction can be seen in terms either of the oxidizing agent or the reducing agent. An oxidizing agent causes the oxidation of another substance by accepting electrons from that substance. A reducing agent causes reduction by providing electrons to another substance.

7.4 Three redox reactions are direct combination, decomposition, and single-replacement reactions. Two or more elements combine to form a single compound in a direct combination reaction. A compound breaks down to form free elements in a decomposition reaction. A free element becomes an ion, and another ion becomes a free element in a single-replacement reaction.

7.5 Redox reactions has many practical applications, such as bleaching, combustion, photography, as well as in preventing corrosion, which is a type of redox reaction.

7.6 Redox reactions can be balanced by making the total increase in oxidation number equal the total decrease.

7.7 Redox reactions can be used to produce electric current in voltaic cells. The negatively charged electrode in a voltaic cell is called the anode, and the positively charged electrode is the cathode.

7.8 The principle of cell potential can be used to compare the strengths of oxidation and reduction reactions. The cell potential is the sum of the oxidation and reduction electrode potentials.

7.9 Batteries are voltaic cells that use redox reactions to produce electricity. Rechargeable batteries are based on reversible redox reactions.

7.10 Electrolysis uses an outside source of electric power to drive nonspontaneous redox reactions.

7. Summary of Key Concepts (continued)

Review Key Terms

On the line provided, write the term from the list that matches each description.

activity series	electrolysis	oxidizing agent
anode	electroplating	redox reaction
cathode	half-cell	reducing agent
cell potential	oxidation	reduction
electrode	oxidation number	voltaic cell

_____ **1.** paired oxidation and reduction reactions

_____ **2.** gives up electrons

_____ **3.** electrochemical cell in which spontaneous redox reactions produce electricity

_____ **4.** gain of electrons

_____ **5.** generates electricity through redox reaction

_____ **6.** site of oxidation or reduction in a cell

_____ **7.** positive electrode in a voltaic cell

_____ **8.** takes away electrons

_____ **9.** loss of electrons

_____ **10.** deposition of metal in an electrolytic cell

_____ **11.** electrode at which oxidation occurs in a cell

_____ **12.** container for substance either to be oxidized or reduced to produce electricity

_____ **13.** ability of a redox reaction in a voltaic cell to move electrons through a wire

_____ **14.** charge of atom if electrons belonged entirely to most electronegative atom

_____ **15.** list of metals in order of reactivity

7. Summary of Key Concepts (continued)

Assess Your Knowledge

Circle the letter of the answer that best completes the sentence or answers the question.

1. A gain in electrons is
   a. what an oxidizing agent causes in another substance.
   b. the overall effect of a redox reaction.
   c. what happens to a reducing agent.
   d. shown by an increase in an atom's oxidation number.

2. The oxidation number of silver in a compound is
   a. $+1$.
   b. $+2$.
   c. -1.
   d. -2.

3. In a decomposition reaction,
   a. elements are oxidized.
   b. elements are reduced.
   c. decay occurs, but no chemical change occurs.
   d. one element is reduced and another is oxidized.

4. In the reaction
   $Ba(NO_3)_2$ (*aq*) + H_2SO_4 (*aq*) → $Ba\ SO_4$ (*s*) + 2 HNO_3 (*aq*)
   a. the oxidation number of Ba changes from $+2$ to $+1$.
   b. there is no change in oxidation numbers.
   c. the oxidation number of S changes from $+2$ to $+1$.
   d. the oxidation number of N changes from $+2$ to $+1$.

5. In a common dry cell
   a. oxygen is oxidized.
   b. nitrogen is reduced.
   c. manganese is oxidized.
   d. zinc is oxidized.

7. *Summary of Key Concepts* (continued)

6. In the reaction for a nickel-cadmium battery,
    $2 Ni(OH)_3 + Cd \rightarrow 2 Ni(OH)_2 + Cd(OH)_2$
    a. nickel is reduced.
    b. nickel is oxidized.
    c. cadmium is reduced.
    d. cadmium is both oxidized and reduced.

7. In a voltaic cell, oxidation takes place at the
    a. wire.
    b. cathode.
    c. anode.
    d. salt bridge.

8. An electric current is used to deposit metal on an object in
    a. electroplating.
    b. recharging.
    c. corrosion.
    d. electrolysis.

9. Which of the following characteristics are likely to be true of a good reducing agent?
    a. does not give up electrons easily
    b. resists burning
    c. has low electronegativity
    d. forms weak bonds with oxygen

10. The cell potential of a voltaic cell is the sum of the contributions from the
    a. oxidation numbers of all elements in the cell.
    b. oxidation reaction at the anode and the reduction reaction at the cathode.
    c. acids and bases in solution.
    d. oxidation numbers of the metals in the activity series.

8. Kinetics and Thermodynamics

Introduction and Key Concepts

In the engine of a car, gasoline and oxygen react explosively to release energy used to power the car. Based on what you have learned so far in chemistry, do you think the products of this reaction could easily be made to react with each other to form gasoline and oxygen again? Explain your answer.

_____

_____

_____

You will need your response to help you review what you have learned by the end of Essential 8.

8.1 How can reaction rates be measured?

Knowing the speed of a chemical reaction is important for being able to control and use it. The area of chemistry concerned with the speed at which reactions occur is called **chemical kinetics.** The speed, or rate, of any event is measured by the amount of change that occurs during a given interval of time. How can the rate of a chemical reaction be measured?

During a chemical reaction, reactants are changed into products, but this does not happen instantaneously. At any time during a reaction, both reactants and products exist in some amount. It makes sense to measure the rate of a chemical reaction, or the **reaction rate,** as the rate at which reactants disappear and products appear.

The amount of reactants and products is better described as the concentration of reactants and products. Concentration is the quantity of a substance in a given volume. The reaction rate is therefore the change in the concentrations of reactants and products during a certain amount of time. Because concentration is expressed in terms of molarity, or moles per kilogram of solvent, the unit used to measure reaction rates is usually molarity per second (M/s). The general equation for any reaction rate can be written as follows.

average rate of reaction =

$$\frac{\text{change in concentration}}{\text{change in time}}$$

The reaction rate must be determined experimentally. It can be found in the laboratory by measuring the concentration of a reactant or product at various times throughout the reaction. The reaction rate cannot be found just by looking at the amounts of reactants and products on each side of the balanced chemical equation for the reaction. In order to see why the reaction rate can only be found experimentally, you must first understand in greater detail what actually happens during a chemical reaction.

8.2 What happens during a chemical reaction?

The rearrangement of atoms that takes place during a chemical reaction is often a complicated process. Even when a reaction can be represented with a relatively simple chemical equation, the reaction does not necessarily occur in one step. Many reactions involve several steps that do not appear in the balanced equation for the reaction. A series of steps leading from reactants to products is called a **reaction mechanism.**

When you set up a chemical reaction in the laboratory or at home, you observe only the overall, or net, chemical change. The reaction

8. Kinetics and Thermodynamics (continued)

mechanism shows the order in which bonds break and atoms are rearranged over the entire course of a chemical reaction. Chemists have been able to devise experiments that reveal the sequence of steps in reaction mechanisms. Each individual reaction step, or **elementary step,** is usually a simple process. Consider the following chemical equation.

$$2 \text{ NO } (g) + \text{F}_2 (g) \rightarrow 2 \text{ NOF } (g)$$

Although it appears from the equation that 2 molecules of NO react with 1 molecule of F_2, that is not what actually happens. Chemists have found that this reaction involves two elementary steps rather than taking place in one step. In the first step, 1 molecule of NO reacts with 1 molecule of F_2 to produce NOF_2.

Step 1: $\text{NO } (g) + \text{F}_2 (g) \rightarrow \text{NOF}_2 (g)$

The product of this first step, NOF_2, then becomes a reactant in the second elementary step. In the second step, NOF_2 reacts with the remaining molecule of NO to form NOF, as shown in the following equation.

Step 2: $\text{NOF}_2 (g) + \text{NO } (g) \rightarrow 2 \text{ NOF } (g)$

The elementary steps in a multistep reaction mechanism must always result in the chemical equation of the overall process. Substances that are produced in one step of a reaction but consumed, or used up, in a later step are called **intermediate products,** or intermediates. In the example above, NOF_2 is the intermediate product. Multistep reaction mechanisms involve one or more intermediate products.

Knowing about reaction mechanisms helps to explain why the rate of a chemical reaction must be found experimentally and cannot be determined from a chemical equation. The reason is that a chemical equation for the overall reaction does not show the elementary steps Each elementary step proceeds at its own rate. One step might proceed quickly while another might proceed slowly. The rate of the overall reaction cannot be faster than the rate of the slowest elementary step. Therefore, the slowest

elementary step is called the **rate-determining step.** The rate of the net, or overall, reaction is dependent on the rates of the elementary steps, especially the rate-determining one.

8.3 How can the reaction rate be determined for given concentrations of reactants?

A **rate law** is an equation that can be used to calculate the reaction rate for any given concentration of reactants. The rate law can be determined by keeping the concentrations of all but one reactant constant, or unchanging, while measuring the reaction rate of that reactant at several different concentrations. The measurements are repeated for each reactant.

The equation for any reaction rate is

$$\text{rate} = k[\text{A}]^x[\text{B}]^y$$

In this equation, [A] and [B] stand for the molar concentrations of a reactant A and a reactant B in moles/liter (M). The exponents x and y are the powers of the concentrations of the reactants. Remember that [A] and [B] are actual numbers, and so it makes sense that they can have exponents. For all reactions, x and y must be determined experimentally. The proportionality constant, k, called a rate constant, has a fixed value for a given reaction at a particular temperature. The proportionality constant must also be determined experimentally. The rate equation can be extended to include reactants C, D, and so on.

8.4 What must happen for a reaction to occur?

Chemists have proposed a theoretical model known as **collision theory,** which helps explain what must happen in order for a reaction to occur. Collision theory is based on the idea that in order for a molecule, atom, or ion to react it must collide either with another molecule, atom, or ion, or with a wall of the container.

8. Kinetics and Thermodynamics (continued)

Billions of collisions can occur without a reaction taking place. This is because not all collisions lead to the formation of products. A collision is an **effective collision** only if it leads to the formation of products. If every collision led to a reaction, chemical reactions would have rates hundreds of time faster than they actually are. The reaction of H_2 and I_2 to form HI proceeds quite slowly, for example, because only about 1 in every 10^{13} collisions (1 followed by 13 zeros) is effective, although each molecule undergoes about 10^{10} collisions every second.

The orientation and energy of the colliding particles are the two factors that determine the effectiveness of a collision. For a reaction to occur, the particles must be oriented in a position that allows the bonds to break and the atoms to rearrange. In 1888, the Swedish chemist Svante Arrhenius suggested that particles must possess a certain minimum amount of kinetic energy in order to react. Kinetic energy is energy of motion, such as the energy of a soccer ball flying through the air or of a rapidly moving train. Particles have kinetic energy because they are constantly moving.

The kinetic energy needed for a reaction to proceed is sometimes compared to a boulder being pushed up and over a bump before rolling down a hill. Even though the boulder will be more stable at the bottom of the hill, it needs a push to get up and over the bump first. Once over the bump, the boulder may roll downhill on its own.

Energy diagrams are graphs that are used to show the changes in energy that occur during a chemical reaction. Energy diagrams usually show high points that resemble the top of a hill. Such high points are called energy barriers. They represent the amount of kinetic energy that the reactants must have before the products will be formed.

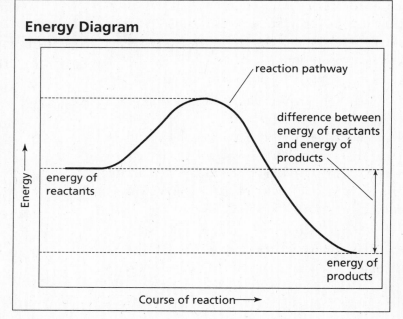

Energy Diagram

reaction pathway

difference between energy of reactants and energy of products

energy of reactants

energy of products

Course of reaction →

Energy →

The energy of the reactants must be raised to the top of the energy barrier before it can drop to a lower level. The difference between the energy at the peak and the energy of the reactants is called the **activation energy** of the reaction. The activation energy is the energy needed to start the reaction.

8.5 How are new bonds formed in a reaction?

New bonds are formed during the **transition state,** an extremely brief period of time when bonds are disrupted and new bonds are formed during a reaction. During the transition state, the reactants form a short-lived complex, called an **activated complex,** that is neither reactant nor product, but has bonds that partially resemble those of both the reactant and the product. The activated complex exists at the point during the reaction when the kinetic energy of the reactants

8. Kinetics and Thermodynamics (continued)

is greatest. This energy peak, called the activation energy, E_a, is the energy required to achieve the transition state and form the activated complex. Because of the short lifetime of an activated complex, chemists cannot actually isolate one for study.

The activated complex is extremely unstable and quickly breaks up in one of two ways. It may form the original bonds again and separate back into the reactant particles, or it may form new bonds and separate into products. The formation of products and the formation of reactants are equally likely to occur.

Be careful not to confuse the activated complex, which is unstable, with the relatively stable intermediate products of the elementary steps of a reaction mechanism. The activated complex, unlike intermediate products, is a very short-lived molecular complex in which bonds are in the process of being broken and formed. Intermediate products, on the other hand, are chemical substances produced in one part of a reaction and consumed in another.

8.6 What makes each reaction occur at a different rate?

Different reactions occur at different rates because they require different amounts of energy. Reactant particles must not only collide at the proper orientation, they must also acquire enough energy to overcome the activation energy barrier in order to be converted into products. Only a small fraction of reactant particles has sufficient energy to overcome the barrier at any given time during the reaction. The reaction rate is the rate at which reactant particles move over the energy barrier.

Every reaction has its own activation energy. Reaction rate is directly related to activation energy. The higher the activation energy, the smaller the fraction of collisions with sufficient energy for the reactants to be converted into products, and the slower the reaction rate will be.

Five general factors affect the rate of a reaction. These factors are nature of reactants themselves, temperature, concentration, surface area, and presence of catalysts. The effect of each factor can be understood in terms of collision theory.

The rate of a reaction depends on how complex the bonds are that have to be broken or formed in order for the reaction to take place. Reactions in which there are only slight rearrangements of atoms are usually rapid at room temperature. Reactions in which there are many covalent bonds to be broken usually take place slowly at room temperature. Whether a reactant is in gaseous, liquid, or solid state in a chemical reaction can also have a considerable effect on reaction rate. Reactions between gases are faster than between liquids—which in turn are usually faster than reactions between solids.

Temperature has an enormous effect on reaction rate. The higher the temperature, the faster the average speed of a group of molecules. The faster the molecules are moving, the more frequently they will collide. Increasing the temperature increases the frequency of collisions and also the fraction of collisions that have enough energy to be effective. Because effective collisions depend on the colliding particles having enough kinetic energy to get over the activation energy barrier, increasing the temperature nearly always increases the reaction rate. The standard rule of thumb that chemists keep in mind is that a 10°C increase in temperature approximately doubles or triples the reaction rate. The exact amount must be determined experimentally, however.

An increase in concentration also causes an increase in reaction rate. An increase in concentration means that there are more particles within a given volume and thus smaller spaces between the reacting particles. With less distance to travel between collisions, more collisions will take place during any given amount of time. Therefore, an increase in

8. *Kinetics and Thermodynamics* (continued)

concentration increases the frequency of the collisions. This can be compared to a room filled with people. The more people in the room, the easier it is for them to bump into each other.

The larger the surface area of a reactant, the greater the number of particles that are exposed for reactions. In other words, the larger surface area increases the frequency at which particles collide. If particles collide more often, the chances for effective collisions increase.

A sample of sugar exposed to oxygen in the air can last for centuries. In the human body, however, sugar exposed to oxygen is consumed in a few seconds. The much higher reaction rate is due to the action of **catalysts.** A catalyst is a substance that increases the rate of the reaction without itself being used up in the reaction. Catalysts act in one or more steps of a reaction by lowering the activation energy. With a lower activation energy, more collisions will have sufficient energy to pass over the energy barrier, as shown in the reaction diagram below.

Catalysts Lower the Activation Energy of Reactions

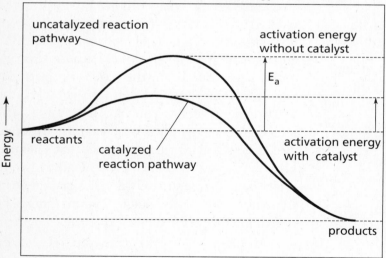

The reaction mechanism of a catalyzed reaction has one step in which the catalyst is consumed and another step in which it is released and made available again. In other

words, catalysts can be recovered and reused after the reaction is complete. Catalysts used in the cells of living things are called **enzymes.** Enzymes increase the speed of reactions that are essential to life and which would be hopelessly slow if the enzymes were not present.

8.7 *What is a spontaneous reaction?*

A process that proceeds on its own, without any outside intervention, is called a spontaneous process. The flow of a river from the mountains to the ocean is a spontaneous process. The melting of ice is an example of a spontaneous physical change. The rusting of iron is an example of a **spontaneous chemical reaction.**

Be careful not to confuse the word *spontaneous* with the words *instantaneous* and *explosive*. The word *instantaneous* refers to the speed, or rate, of a process. A spontaneous process may be so rapid that it is instantaneous, but it may also be so slow that the products are not detected even after thousands of years. Although all explosive reactions are spontaneous, most spontaneous reactions are not explosive.

It is often possible for the products of a reaction to react in a reverse reaction to form the reactants. However, reactions tend to proceed in one direction more readily than in the other. For example, the iron in a brand new nail that has been left outside will react with oxygen in the air to form rust, but a rusty nail will not on its own turn back into a shiny new nail. The spontaneous direction of a given reaction and the extent to which the reaction will proceed (K_{eq}) are a part of the subject of thermodynamics.

8. Kinetics and Thermodynamics (continued)

8.8 How can the spontaneous direction of a reaction be determined?

The spontaneity of a reaction depends upon the change in **enthalpy** of the reaction. The enthalpy of a substance, for all practical purposes, represents the energy of the substance. The difference in enthalpies of reactants compared to their products is the difference in their energies. The enthalpy of products (H_p) minus the enthalpy of reactants (H_r) is called the ΔH, or change in enthalpy, for a reaction.

Some reactions release heat and some absorb it. A reaction that releases heat is an exothermic reaction, and a reaction that absorbs heat is an endothermic reaction. The change in enthalpy (ΔH) for an exothermic reaction is defined as being negative and the ΔH for an endothermic reaction is positive.

An exothermic reaction can be visualized as one in which reactants roll down a potential energy "hill" to become products at the bottom of the hill. The potential energy is released in the form of heat as they roll down the hill. Remember that potential energy is stored energy. An exothermic reaction releases energy stored in the bonds of the reactants. Most exothermic reactions are spontaneous. Although most spontaneous process are exothermic, some are endothermic. How can both exothermic reactions and endothermic reactions be spontaneous?

The reason is that enthalpy is not the only factor that determines whether a process is spontaneous or not. Disorder also plays an important role in determining which reactions will proceed spontaneously. As a way of describing and comparing the disorder present in various substances and situations, the thermodynamic concept of **entropy** was invented. Entropy is a quantitative measure of the disorder, or randomness, in the substances involved in a reaction. Entropy is given the symbol S. The greater the disorder, the larger the value of S.

As ice melts into water, molecules of H_2O arranged in an ordered crystalline pattern as solid ice become liquid water, which is more disordered. Because ice absorbs heat from its surroundings, melting ice is an example of a spontaneous endothermic process. In all spontaneous endothermic chemical reactions the products are more disordered than the reactants.

When a reaction occurs, there is an accompanying change in entropy. The entropy of products minus the entropy of reactants is defined as the entropy change for a reaction, as the following equation shows.

$$\Delta S = S_{products} - S_{reactants}$$

When the entropy of the products is greater than the entropy of the reactants ($S_{products} > S_{reactants}$), the change in entropy, ΔS, is said to be positive. In such reactions, entropy increases and the products have more disorder than the reactants.

Entropy increases when
- gases are formed from liquids and solids.
- solutions are formed from liquids and solids.
- there are more molecules of gas as products than there are as reactants.
- the temperature of a substance is increased.

A very important law of thermodynamics states that in any spontaneous process, the overall entropy always increases. You have probably already observed that things in general tend to become more disordered when left alone, just as your room at home does as soon as you stop making an effort to keep it clean and neat. This thermodynamic law refers not to the entropy change for the reaction alone, but rather to the overall entropy change in the reaction and its surroundings considered as a whole, which chemists call the "universe." The change in the

8. Kinetics and Thermodynamics (continued)

entropy of the universe is the sum of the entropy change for the reaction itself plus the entropy change for the surroundings. That idea can be expressed using the following equation.

$$\Delta S_{universe} = \Delta S_{reaction} + \Delta S_{surroundings}$$

A reaction is spontaneous when the entropy change of the universe ($\Delta S_{universe}$) is positive; that is, when the sum on the right side of the above equation is greater than zero.

A change in enthalpy (ΔH) can cause a change in entropy (ΔS). The entropy of the surroundings increases or decreases as heat is released or absorbed by a reaction. An exothermic reaction heats up its surroundings and thereby increases the entropy of its surroundings. On the other hand, an endothermic reaction cools its surroundings, decreasing its entropy. What happens if the changes in enthalpy and entropy oppose each other? In which direction will the spontaneous reaction be? When these two factors oppose each other, the spontaneous direction of the reaction depends on which factor is greater.

The American mathematician J. Willard Gibbs proposed a thermodynamic concept to combine the concepts of entropy and enthalpy. He called this concept free energy. It is now called **Gibbs free energy** in his honor and is given the symbol G. Just as with enthalpy and entropy, chemists are mostly interested in knowing the *change* in Gibbs free energy (ΔG) of a reaction. This change equals the enthalpy change (ΔH) for the reaction minus the product of the absolute temperature (in kelvins) and the reaction's entropy change ($T\Delta S$), as expressed in the following equation.

$$\Delta G = \Delta H - T\Delta S$$

The change in Gibbs free energy (ΔG) can be used to predict whether a reaction will proceed spontaneously or not. The following statements summarize how to determine the spontaneous direction of a reaction.

- If ΔG is negative, the reaction is spontaneous and can proceed on its own.
- If ΔG is positive, the reaction is not spontaneous and requires energy from outside to make it occur.
- If ΔG is zero, the reaction is at equilibrium.

8.9 Can energy from reactions be harnessed to do work?

Gibbs free energy is a measure of the maximum amount of energy available in a system to do work. Gibbs free energy always decreases in a spontaneous process. The change in the Gibbs free energy determines the maximum work that a spontaneous process can perform. It is also the minimum work required to carry out a nonspontaneous process. If the change in Gibbs free energy is zero, the system is at equilibrium.

A spontaneous reaction—a reaction that proceeds on its own—can be harnessed to do work because spontaneous reactions release free energy ($\Delta G_{negative}$) that can perform work. For example, when gasoline is burned in the engine of a car, the free energy released during the oxidation reaction is harnessed to deliver power to the wheels. However, this work can never exceed the magnitude or size of ΔG for the reaction. In other words, the free energy change, ΔG, represents the maximum work that a spontaneous process can perform in a perfectly efficient system.

This explains the origin of the name free energy. The word *free* refers to the portion of the total energy change of a spontaneous process that is available to do useful work. The remainder is unavailable—it has been "lost" to the environment because the entropy of the reaction and its surroundings must always increase. This is an important consequence of the thermodynamic law because it tells us that although the total energy of the universe is constant, the energy is continually being dispersed so that it is not as useful for doing work.

8. *Summary of Key Concepts*

At the beginning of Essential 8, you were asked if the products of combustion in a car's engine could easily react to form gasoline and oxygen again. Read your statements again, and in the space below add to them or change them based on what you have learned in Essential 8. Then review the key concepts below.

_____

_____

_____

8.1 The rate of a reaction is a measure of how quickly reactants turn into products. This rate must be determined experimentally by measuring the change in concentration of a reactant or product as the reaction proceeds. Chemical kinetics is the area of chemistry concerned with reaction rates.

8.2 Most chemical reactions proceed through a series of simple reactions, or elementary steps. The series of steps is called the reaction mechanism. Substances that are produced in one elementary step and consumed in another are called intermediate products. The rate-determining step is the elementary step that determines the rate of the overall reaction.

8.3 A rate law for a chemical reaction describes the relationship between the concentrations of the reactants and the reaction rate.

8.4 Collision theory is based on the assumption that particles must collide at the proper orientation and with sufficient kinetic energy in order to react. Collisions leading to formation of products are called effective collisions. The energy of the reactants must first reach the activation energy before the collisions become effective and the reaction can proceed.

8.5 The activated complex is formed during the transition state at the peak energy of a reaction. Bonds in the activated complex resemble those of both reactant and product. The activated complex is unstable and quickly either goes forward to form the product or backward to form the reactant again.

8.6 Factors affecting the rate at which a reaction proceeds are: the nature of the reactants, the temperature at which the reaction occurs, the surface areas of reactants exposed to each other, the concentration of the reactants present, and the presence of catalysts.

8.7 A spontaneous process is one that proceeds on its own without any outside intervention.

8.8 The enthalpy of a substance is a measure of its total energy. Changes in enthalpy represent the heat transferred in chemical and physical processes. Most exothermic reactions are spontaneous. Entropy is a measure of the disorder present in a given substance or system. Gases have the highest energy, solids have the lowest entropy, and liquids have moderate entropy. In any spontaneous process, the entropy of the universe always increases.

8.9 Gibbs free energy always decreases in a spontaneous process. The change in the Gibbs free energy is the maximum work that a spontaneous process can perform, and the minimum work required to carry out a nonspontaneous process.

8. Summary of Key Concepts (continued)

Review Key Terms

On the line provided, write the term from the list that matches each description.

activated complex

activation energy

catalyst

effective collision

elementary step

enthalpy

entropy

Gibbs free energy

intermediate product

rate law

reaction mechanism

spontaneous process

_____ **1.** energy that is available for doing work

_____ **2.** substance produced but later consumed in a multistep reaction

_____ **3.** energy barrier that must be exceeded for reaction to proceed

_____ **4.** equation used to calculate reaction rate based on concentrations of products and reactants

_____ **5.** measure of the total energy of a substance

_____ **6.** one step in a multistep reaction

_____ **7.** process that proceeds on its own

_____ **8.** measure of the disorder in a substance or system

_____ **9.** substance that lowers a reaction's activation energy without being consumed

_____ **10.** collision between particles to form products

_____ **11.** series of steps in an overall chemical reaction

_____ **12.** short-lived substance resembling both reactants and products

8. Summary of Key Concepts (continued)

Assess Your Knowledge
Circle the letter of the response that best completes the sentence or answers the question.

1. Change in enthalpy is represented by the symbol
   a. ΔH.
   b. ΔS.
   c. ΔG.
   d. ΔE.

2. An endothermic reaction
   a. usually increases the entropy of its surroundings.
   b. is always a spontaneous process.
   c. absorbs heat.
   d. raises the temperature of its surroundings.

3. A temporary substance, neither reactant nor product, formed during the transition state in a reaction, is a(n)
   a. intermediate product.
   b. catalyst.
   c. activated complex.
   d. inhibitor.

4. The rate of a chemical reaction can be increased by
   a. increasing the temperature of the reactants.
   b. adding catalysts.
   c. increasing the concentrations of reactants.
   d. all of the above.

5. When ΔG is 0,
   a. the reaction is at equilibrium.
   b. the reaction is spontaneous.
   c. the reaction is nonspontaneous.
   d. products are favored.

8. *Summary of Key Concepts* (continued)

6. Which of the following statements is false?
   a. Entropy increases when gases are formed from liquids and solids.
   b. Entropy increases when solutions are formed from liquids and solids.
   c. Entropy increases when the rate of a reaction increases.
   d. Entropy increases when the temperature of a substance is increased.

7. Which equation best expresses the idea of Gibbs free energy?
   a. rate $= k[A]^x[B]^y$
   b. $\Delta S = S_{products} - S_{reactants}$
   c. $\Delta S_{universe} = \Delta S_{reaction} + \Delta S_{surroundings}$
   d. $\Delta G = \Delta H - T\Delta S$

8. A substance that allows reactions to take place more quickly in the cells of living things is called an
   a. activated complex.
   b. enzyme.
   c. intermediate product.
   d. effective collision.

9. The activated complex in a reaction is a(n)
   a. intermediate product in a reaction that has several elementary steps.
   b. molecular complex in which bonds are in the process of being broken or formed.
   c. stable substance produced in one part of a reaction and consumed in another.
   d. substance that makes the reaction more active without being used up in the reaction.

10. A reaction will proceed spontaneously when $\Delta H - T\Delta S$ is
    a. equal to 0.
    b. equal to ΔG.
    c. greater than 0.
    d. less than 0.

9. Nuclear Chemistry

Introduction and Key Concepts

Two chemistry students are having a disagreement. One student claims that reactions exist in which an atom of one element becomes an atom of a different element. The other student disagrees, believing instead that although the electrons of atoms take part in reactions, the atoms themselves remain the same. Whose idea is correct? Explain your thinking, based on what you have learned so far in chemistry. Write your statements in the space below.

_____

_____

_____

You will need your response to review what you have learned at the end of Essential 9.

9.1 What is radioactivity?

In chemical reactions, atoms interact only through their outer electrons, while their nuclei remain unchanged. Nuclear reactions are different from chemical reactions, however. A nuclear reaction changes the composition, or makeup, of an atom's nucleus. During a nuclear reaction, atoms spontaneously emit, or release, alpha particles, beta particles, or gamma rays. These three kinds of emission are called radiation. Elements that emit radiation are said to be **radioactive.**

Most atoms found in the everyday world are not radioactive. In other words, most atoms in our environment have stable nuclei. In a stable nucleus, an attractive force acting within the atomic nucleus, called the **strong nuclear force,** overcomes the electrical repulsion force between the protons and keeps the protons in the nucleus from flying apart. The strong nuclear force is one of the strongest forces known in nature, but it is important only at the extremely short distances found in the nuclei of atoms. Neutrons exert strong nuclear force, which is an attractive force, but because they are electrically neutral they do not exert a force of repulsion. For that reason, neutrons serve as a "glue" that holds the nucleus together.

For elements with atomic numbers between 1 and 20 (from hydrogen to calcium), stable nuclei have almost equal numbers of protons and neutrons. Beyond 20 protons, nuclei need increasingly more neutrons than protons to be stable. When the atomic number is greater than 83 (the element bismuth), no number of neutrons is enough to glue the nucleus firmly together. Therefore, all nuclei with atomic numbers greater than 83 are radioactive.

Unstable nuclei may emit alpha, beta, or gamma radiation. The words *alpha*, *beta*, and *gamma* have the symbols α, β, and γ, respectively, which are the first three letters of the Greek alphabet. The names of the three types of radiation can be abbreviated by using these Greek letters.

Alpha particles have a 2+ charge, or a charge twice that of an electron but with the opposite sign. Like atoms, radiation can be represented by symbols. An alpha particle is represented by the symbol $_2^4\alpha$, showing that an alpha particle consists of 2 protons and 2 neutrons. It can also be represented as $_2^4He$ because it is identical to a helium atom that has a mass number of 4.

Beta particles are high-speed electrons. A beta radiation is represented by $_{-1}^0e$, or by $_{-1}^0\beta$. The top number shows that the mass number is zero, and this is true because an electron has an extremely small mass compared to a proton or a neutron. The bottom number shows that the particle has a charge of 1–.

9. Nuclear Chemistry (continued)

Gamma radiation is a very energetic form of light, and is similar to X-rays. A gamma ray does not consist of particles, so it is symbolized by $_0^0\gamma$. Heavy lead shielding is needed to stop gamma rays, which can penetrate deep into the body and cause serious tissue damage.

Not only are nuclei unstable if they contain too few neutrons, they are also unstable if they contain too many neutrons. Nuclei that have too many neutrons are likely to emit beta radiation. In the process that produces beta radiation, a neutron changes into a proton and an electron. The proton remains in the nucleus, and the electron—or beta particle—is propelled out of the nucleus at high speed.

When an atom emits alpha, beta, or gamma radiation, it is said to be undergoing radioactive decay. During radioactive decay, the original nucleus decomposes, or decays, to form a new nucleus, releasing radiation in the process.

9.2 Do all atoms of an element have the same number of neutrons?

Remember that when atoms of an element have the same number of protons but different numbers of neutrons, the different types of atoms are called isotopes of that element. Many elements have a least one naturally occurring radioactive isotope, or **radioisotope.** In nature, elements are almost always found as a mixture of isotopes. Remember that the mass number is the sum of the number of protons and neutrons. Therefore, each isotope of an element has a different mass number. To write the name of an isotope using chemical symbols, place the mass number above the atomic number. For example, the symbol for carbon-14 is $_6^{14}C$. You can find the number of neutrons in an isotope by subtracting the atomic number from the mass number.

The decay of unstable isotopes is a spontaneous process that takes place continuously. All elements have one or more isotopes that are unstable and that decay to produce other elements. These elements may be natural, or they may only exist in a laboratory. Many elements have at least one radioisotope that occurs naturally.

The time it takes for one half of a sample of a radioisotope to decay is called the **half-life** of that radioisotope. For example, the half-life of the radioisotope carbon-14 is 5730 years. This means that after 5730 years, one half of the ^{14}C in a particular sample would be gone. If you start with a 1.000-gram sample, only 0.500 g would be left after 5730 years. After 11,460 years (5730 + 5730), only one quarter, or 0.250 g, of the original sample is left.

9.3 How can radioactivity be used to estimate the age of plant or animal remains?

Carbon-14 is commonly used in estimating the age of plant and animal remains. Cosmic rays, which are streams of high-energy charged particles from outer space, act on the Earth's upper atmosphere to produce carbon-14. After being produced by the cosmic rays, the carbon-14 is oxidized to form $^{14}CO_2$, which then mixes with the ordinary $^{12}CO_2$ already in the atmosphere. As a result, the atmosphere always has a certain amount of both $^{14}CO_2$ and $^{12}CO_2$. The amounts of each are relatively constant.

Green plants take in carbon dioxide for use in photosynthesis. Photosynthesis is the process by which green plants use the sun's energy to convert carbon dioxide and water into sugars and starches. The sugars and starches, in turn, are food for animals that eat the plants. The amount of carbon-14 isotope is constant in plants and animals while they are alive, but carbon-14 stops being taken into plant or animal tissue once the organism dies.

The beta radiation emitted by the carbon-14 in the plant or animal remains can be measured. By determining the rate of beta emission

9. Nuclear Chemistry *(continued)*

scientists can calculate how much time has passed since the plant or animal died by comparing the amount of radioactive carbon-14 with the amount of stable carbon-12. The emission of beta particles drops as the carbon-14 decays. After 5730 years the rate of beta emission will have dropped to one half the rate in living organisms; after 11,460 years the rate will have dropped to one quarter, and so on. The age of objects made of plant or animal products, such as wood, textiles, or leather can also be estimated using this method of carbon-14 dating.

9.4 How can stable nuclei be made unstable?

One way to make a stable nucleus become unstable is with a nuclear bombardment reaction. In a **nuclear bombardment reaction,** a stream of particles, such as alpha particles, is directed at the nucleus of an atom. When these particles strike the nucleus, they can combine with the nucleus to form a new nucleus, producing a new element.

Ernest Rutherford was the first scientist to discover nuclear bombardment reactions. In 1919, he observed that when a high-speed alpha particle strikes a nitrogen-14 nucleus, the reaction produces oxygen-17 and hydrogen-1. The nuclear reaction can be represented by the following nuclear reaction equation.

$$\,^{4}_{2}\alpha + \,^{14}_{7}N \rightarrow \,^{17}_{8}O + \,^{1}_{1}H$$

In equations for nuclear reactions, the mass numbers and the atomic numbers must balance on each side of the arrow. Just as in chemical reactions, matter is neither created nor destroyed in a nuclear reaction.

Using alpha particles to change one element into another is not easy to do. Because both a nucleus and an alpha particle carry a positive charge and like charges repel each other, an alpha particle is deflected away from the nucleus. For an alpha particle to overcome this force of repulsion and physically collide with a nucleus, it must have a large amount of kinetic energy. In other words, for a successful nuclear bombardment reaction to take place, an alpha particle must be moving extremely fast.

Scientists have developed many types of devices for accelerating alpha particles and other particles fast enough to collide with a nucleus and cause a nuclear reaction. These devices are called particle accelerators, but they are sometimes known as "atom smashers."

9.5 Is radioactivity harmful to living things?

Only a few elements encountered in everyday life are naturally radioactive. This is fortunate, because radiation is harmful to living things. The amount of damage caused by radiation depends on the amount and type of radiation to which a living organism is exposed.

Alpha particles are usually not a hazard to humans because they are easily stopped, even by clothing. Beta particles are more penetrating and can pass through clothing and damage the skin. Gamma rays are similar to X-rays and are extremely penetrating. Heavy shielding made of lead is needed to stop gamma rays.

Highly penetrating radiation has enough energy to strip electrons from molecules to form ions. These ions are so reactive that they easily disrupt the vital functioning of living cells. This can lead to the destruction of tissues. Leukemia, for example, can be caused by radiation.

$$\,^{4}_{2}\alpha \qquad \,^{14}_{7}N \qquad \,^{17}_{8}O \qquad \,^{1}_{1}H$$

Nuclear Bombardment Reaction of Nitrogen-14 to Produce Oxygen-17 and a Proton

9. Nuclear Chemistry *(continued)*

There are two ways in which radiation may damage an organism. Radiation damage may affect an organism directly or it may affect the organism's offspring. Radiation affects an organism's offspring by damaging reproductive cells. Damage caused to reproductive cells may adversely affect the development of offspring.

9.6 How can radiation be measured?

Because of the dangers of radiation, being able to detect radiation in the environment is important. The **Geiger counter** is the most common instrument for detecting radiation. A Geiger counter consists of a hollow cylinder filled with argon gas. Alpha, beta, or gamma particles ionize the argon gas as they pass through the cylinder. Electrodes in the Geiger counter attract the ions, that then create an electric pulse. This electric pulse is amplified and sent to a counter or recorder. The pulse is also often used to make an audible click over a speaker. As the Geiger counter gets nearer to a source of radioactivity, the clicks occur closer and closer together, indicating that radioactivity is increasing.

Another device used for measuring radioactivity is the **dosimeter.** The dosimeter measures the total amount of radiation to which a person has been exposed. Most dosimeters consist of photographic film that is covered by a layer of material such as paper or plastic. This layer prevents light from reaching the film but allows radiation to pass through. People who risk becoming exposed to too much radiation, such as workers in nuclear power plants, often wear dosimeters as badges. At the end of a work shift, the film is taken out of the dosimeter and developed. The total amount of radiation received by the person who had worn the badge will be revealed by how dark the developed film gets.

9.7 What beneficial uses does radiation have?

In spite of the hazards of radiation, radioisotopes have many beneficial uses in medicine, agriculture, and industry. In medicine, radioactive materials are used as radiotracers and in the treatment of cancer. Radiotracers are sometimes referred to as radioactive labels. They are used for tracking a specific substance as it moves through a patient's body. A very small amount of the substance is replaced by a radioactive isotope of that substance. As the radioactive isotope travels through the patient's body, it can be followed using a Geiger counter. In this way, for example, cobalt-58 is used to trace the body's ability to absorb vitamin B_{12}, which contains cobalt. Iodine-131, a beta emitter with a half-life of 8.1 days, is used to gain information about a patient's thyroid gland, which is the only part of the body that takes up iodine.

Radioisotopes are often used in treating cancer. Cancer is a disease in which cells in the body are produced at a rate much faster than the rate for normal cells. The mass of abnormal tissue resulting from this runaway growth is called a tumor. Tumors are more likely to be destroyed by gamma rays than normal cells are. As a result, radiation therapy can be used to fight the disease. The same radiation that destroys cancer cells can also cause cancer in healthy cells. Therefore, doctors must carefully choose which radioactive isotope to use and how to administer it in order for the radiation therapy to be effective.

Radiotracers are also used in areas besides medicine. For example, barium-140, which is a radioactive form of the insoluble compound barium sulfate ($BaSO_4$), can be used to follow the movement of silt in rivers. Compounds containing radioactive phosphorus-32 have been used to study the uptake of nutrients by plants.

9. Nuclear Chemistry (continued)

Radiation is sometimes also used to preserve certain foods. Strawberries, for example, can be ruined by molds and bacteria. However, those microorganisms are killed by radiation. By exposing fruit to radiation, such as gamma rays from cobalt-60, fruit can remain on the store shelf much longer without spoiling.

9.8 How do nuclear reactions release energy?

Energy released in nuclear reactions is enormously greater than the energy released in chemical reactions. The energy released by the decay of a gram of radioactive atoms, for example, is hundreds of thousands of times greater than the energy released per gram of chemical reactant. However, radioactive decay reactions are not practical as power sources. One nuclear reaction that actually is widely used as a source of power today is the **nuclear fission reaction.**

Nuclear fission was first understood by physicist Lise Meitner (1878–1968). She recognized that in a nuclear fission reaction, a large nucleus splits into two smaller nuclei of approximately equal mass. The word fission means "splitting."

Unlike what happens in chemical reactions, in nuclear fission reactions the amount of mass in the products of the reaction is not the same as the amount of mass in the starting materials. The products have slightly less mass. In other words, the law of conservation of mass does not apply to fission reactions.

What happens to the missing mass? The answer is that it is converted into energy. The amount of energy released can be calculated using Albert Einstein's famous equation: $E = mc^2$. In this equation, E stands for the amount of energy released, m is the mass lost in the reaction, and c is the speed of light (3×10^8, or 300,000,000, meters per second). Even when the amount of mass lost in the reaction is very small, the resulting value for the energy released, E, is extremely large.

A nuclear fission reaction can be produced by bombarding an atom of uranium-235 with a neutron. The uranium atom splits into the lighter elements barium-141 and krypton-92. Three neutrons are also produced, each of which may bombard other uranium-235 atoms to start more fission reactions, which release more neutrons, and so on, in a series of fission reactions called a **nuclear chain reaction.** Once started, a nuclear chain reaction can release an immense amount of energy in a very short time. Atomic bombs were designed to produce a runaway nuclear chain reaction.

9.9 How are nuclear reactions harnessed as sources of power?

Atomic bombs are terribly destructive because they are uncontrolled. However, not all nuclear chain reactions are uncontrolled. The chain reaction that takes place inside a nuclear power plant is regulated by control rods. These rods are inserted between the uranium fuel rods in the core of the reactor. The control rods absorb neutrons and keep the chain reaction from becoming explosive. Heat from the controlled chain reaction taking place in the reactor's core is generally used to produce steam for generating electricity.

Although nuclear reactors are useful as power sources, they are also a source of radioactive waste material that is difficult to dispose of. Radioactive fission products build up in the fuel rods as the fuel undergoes fission reaction and the fissionable material is used up. Eventually the fuel rods must be replaced, and the spent fuel rods are highly radioactive.

Disposal of this radioactive waste is a major problem. Burying it underground is one solution, but people do not agree on where the waste

9. *Nuclear Chemistry* (continued)

should be buried. Until a more risk-free method of nuclear waste disposal is developed, nuclear power will be a controversial source of energy.

A **nuclear fusion reaction** is another type of nuclear reaction that might someday become a source of energy. In a nuclear fusion reaction, two small nuclei combine to form a larger nucleus, releasing energy in the process. The following equation, for example, shows the fusion reaction in which two isotopes of hydrogen combine to form helium and a neutron.

$$^2_1H + ^3_1H \rightarrow ^4_2He + ^1_0n$$

As happens in a fission reaction, a fusion reaction converts some of the mass of the original nuclei into energy. Fusion reactions release large amounts of energy, but unfortunately they are difficult to produce and control. In order for two atoms to fuse, their nuclei must come together. This action is resisted by the repulsion of the atom's negatively charged electron clouds and by the repulsion between the positively charged nuclei.

The electrons of the atoms can be stripped off by raising the hydrogen to very high temperatures until it exists only as a "sea" of bare nuclei, called **plasma,** which is one of the basic phases of matter. The sun and other stars consist of plasma. Plasma must be heated to a temperature of about 40 million kelvins for the nuclei to overcome their repulsion force and fuse with each other. Because of such high temperatures, nuclear fusion reactions are called thermonuclear reactions. (*thermo-* means "heat"). Thermonuclear reactions are the source of the immense energy that the sun and stars release.

Fusion reactions may someday be an important source of energy. A fusion reaction using hydrogen as fuel would release more energy per gram of fuel than does a fission reaction. Also, the products of a fusion reaction are not radioactive. However, the controlled use of fusion is still in the experimental stage because the high temperatures required are very difficult to achieve and maintain.

9. *Summary of Key Concepts*

At the beginning of Essential 9, you were asked whether reactions exist that change one element into another. Read your statements again, and in the space below add to them or change them based on what you have learned in Essential 9. Then review the key concepts below.

_____

_____

_____

9.1 Nuclear reactions change the composition of an atom's nucleus. Unstable nuclei may emit alpha, beta, or gamma radiation. Alpha and beta radiation consist of particles. Gamma radiation is a very energetic form of light. Radioactive elements are elements that emit radiation.

9.2 Many elements have a least one naturally occurring radioactive isotope, or radioisotope. The half-life of a radioisotope is the time it takes for one half of a sample of that isotope to decay.

9.3 Carbon-14 is a radioisotope used in estimating the age of plant and animal remains. Living things take in constant amounts of carbon-14 while they are alive. After they die, the radioactive carbon-14 decays. By measuring the amount of radioactive carbon, scientists can calculate how much time has passed since the plant or animal died.

9.4 In a nuclear bombardment reaction, an atom's nucleus is bombarded with a stream of particles and the nucleus changes into the nucleus of a different element. For a nuclear reaction to take place, the particles must be moving rapidly enough to overcome the repulsion forces exerted by the nucleus.

9.5 Radiation is hazardous to living things. Highly penetrating radiation damages living tissue by ionizing molecules in the tissue.

9.6 The Geiger counter and the dosimeter are devices used for measuring radiation. A Geiger counter works on the basis of the ionizing effect of radiation. A dosimeter uses radiation-sensitive photographic film.

9.7 Radioisotopes have many beneficial applications in medicine as radiotracers and in cancer treatment, as well as in food preservation.

9.8 Two types of nuclear reactions that are effective energy sources are nuclear fission, in which larger nuclei are split into smaller ones, and in nuclear fusion, in which smaller nuclei are fused into larger ones. In these reactions, a small amount of matter is converted into energy. A nuclear fission chain reaction occurs as neutrons from one reaction produce more reactions.

9.9 Nuclear fission reactions can be controlled and harnessed as a source of power. Nuclear fusion reactions may someday be used as a power source, but doing so is hard because fusion reactions require that hydrogen exist as extremely hot plasma, a state of matter in which nuclei have been stripped of electrons.

9. Summary of Key Concepts (continued)

Review Key Terms

On the line provided, write the term from the list that matches each description.

dosimeter
Geiger counter
half-life
nuclear bombardment reaction
nuclear chain reaction
nuclear fission reaction
nuclear fusion reaction
plasma
radioactive
radioisotope
strong nuclear force

_____ **1.** use of a stream of high-speed alpha particles to change an atom's nucleus

_____ **2.** atom with unstable nucleus that emits alpha, beta, or gamma particles

_____ **3.** series of fission reactions producing other fission reactions

_____ **4.** breaking apart of a larger nucleus to form smaller nuclei

_____ **5.** form of an element that can change spontaneously into another element

_____ **6.** joining of smaller nuclei to form a larger nucleus

_____ **7.** uses exposure of film to indicate radiation received

_____ **8.** time it takes for one half of a radioactive sample to decay

_____ **9.** holds neutrons and protons together

_____ **10.** state of matter in which nuclei exist separately from electrons

_____ **11.** measures intensity of radiation based on ionization

9. *Summary of Key Concepts* (continued)

Assess Your Knowledge

Circle the letter of the response that best completes the sentence or answers the question.

1. Nuclear reactions are different from chemical reactions because nuclear reactions
   a. take place in stable nuclei.
   b. involve mainly valence electrons.
   c. are important only at extremely short distances.
   d. involve transformation of nuclei and emission of radioactivity.

2. Gamma radiation is the only type of radiation that
   a. has a charge of 2+.
   b. has a charge of 1−.
   c. consists of high-energy radiation instead of particles.
   d. is emitted during radioactive decay of an unstable nucleus.

3. An alpha particle will collide with a nucleus to produce a nuclear bombardment reaction only when
   a. the positively charged alpha particle is moving fast enough.
   b. the nucleus is unstable enough to decay and produce a lighter nucleus and a proton.
   c. the half-life of the element being bombarded is short enough.
   d. gamma radiation is penetrating enough to strip electrons from molecules to form ions.

4. If the half-life of a radioactive isotope is 500 years, how many years will it take for only one quarter of a certain sample of it to be left?
   a. 125 years
   b. 750 years
   c. 1000 years
   d. 2000 years

5. Which of the following devices is *not* useful for measuring radiation?
   a. a Geiger counter
   b. a dosimeter
   c. a particle accelerator
   d. a radiotracer

6. Radioisotopes cannot yet be used for
   a. healing any types of cancer.
   b. increasing the shelf life of foods.
   c. tracing movement of iodine within the body.
   d. producing inexpensive, safe fuel.

9. *Summary of Key Concepts* (continued)

7. According to Einstein's equation, $E = mc^2$,
   a. a small mass can be converted to a large amount of energy.
   b. a small mass can be converted to a large mass.
   c. a small amount of energy can be converted to a large mass.
   d. a small amount of energy can be converted to a large amount of energy.

8. A commonly used isotope for dating plant and animal remains is
   a. uranium-238.
   b. carbon-14.
   c. carbon-12.
   d. uranium-235.

9. Neutrons contribute to nuclear stability primarily because
   a. they exert a stronger attractive force than the attractive force exerted by positively charged protons in the nucleus.
   b. they exert strong nuclear force, which is attractive, but they are electrically neutral and do not exert repulsive force against protons.
   c. they have a similar mass as protons but they are electrically neutral.
   d. they take up space in the nucleus and prevent protons from repelling each other by keeping them further apart.

10. What may result when reproductive cells are exposed to radiation?
    a. high blood pressure
    b. genetic defects in offspring
    c. cataracts and burns
    d. diabetes

10. Organic Chemistry

Introduction and Key Concepts

Many compounds that are produced by living organisms or that are found in them can also be synthesized by chemists in a laboratory. Are such compounds exactly the same regardless of where or how they are synthesized? Explain your answer based on what you have learned in chemistry so far.

_____

_____

_____

You will need your response to help you review what you have learned by the end of Essential 10.

10.1 What makes carbon special?

Carbon is a unique and amazing element. It may be more important to life than any other element. Carbon atoms form the backbone of almost every molecule that living organisms use or make. Carbon's properties allow it to be a part of an unusually wide variety of compounds.

The element carbon can be found in several different forms such as diamond, graphite, and amorphous carbon. These forms of carbon are called **allotropes.** Each allotrope has a different bonding pattern and different physical properties. While diamond is the hardest substance known on Earth, graphite is the soft substance used to make pencil "lead." Amorphous carbon, found in coal and soot, has no predictable structure.

Carbon is a relatively small atom that has only four valence electrons. Remember that the octet rule says that an atom is most stable when it has eight electrons in its outer level. To satisfy the octet rule, a carbon atom will form four covalent bonds with other atoms. Because carbon is a relatively small atom, its electrons are quite close to the nucleus. This closeness allows the four covalent bonds formed by carbon to be short and strong.

However, carbon atoms differ from other small atoms because carbon does not usually exist in a pair as a diatomic molecule. Instead of forming diatomic molecules, carbon atoms form long chains by bonding with other carbon atoms or with atoms of other elements. These long chains of carbon atoms provide the framework for an enormous variety of compounds, including most of the molecules that living organisms make or use.

A carbon atom forms four covalent bonds with other atoms. These bonds can be single, double, or triple bonds. Depending on whether the bonds formed are single, double, or triple, a carbon atom can bond with 4, 3, or 2 other atoms.

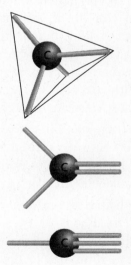

Carbon Atoms Form Single, Double, or Triple Bonds

Until the nineteenth century, living things were thought to contain compounds that could

10. Organic Chemistry (continued)

not be synthesized in the laboratory. These were called organic because they came from living organisms. In 1828, when the German chemist Friedrich Wöhler (1800–1882) synthesized urea (the main component of urine), that theory was challenged. The word *organic* came to mean "containing carbon." Today, an organic molecule is considered to be any molecule that contains carbon, whether that molecule is produced by living things or not, and **organic chemistry** is the study of carbon compounds. Oxides of carbon and carbonates are exceptions. They are considered inorganic because their properties are similar to those of inorganic molecules. Chemists now know that any organic compound can be synthesized in a laboratory.

10.2 What compounds can be formed from only carbon and hydrogen?

A compound consisting entirely of carbon and hydrogen atoms is a **hydrocarbon.** Hydrocarbons are nonpolar molecules that may form straight or branched chains, or rings. Because they can form so many different patterns, and can have different kinds of bonds, they can form a large variety of compounds. Most of these compounds make good fuels because they react with oxygen to produce carbon dioxide and water, releasing energy and light.

Because there is little difference in electronegativity between carbon and hydrogen, the carbon-hydrogen bond is nonpolar, and so hydrocarbon molecules are also nonpolar.

Although hydrocarbons are made of only two elements, thousands of types are possible. This is true because the carbon atoms in a hydrocarbon can form single, double, or triple bonds. Carbons can bond together in chains, which can be either straight chains or branched chains. Carbons can also bond together to form ring-shaped molecules.

Chemists need a way to represent the many possible structures of carbon-based molecules. The molecular formula C_4H_8 tells you that the molecule has 4 carbon atoms and 8 hydrogen atoms. However, the molecular formula says nothing about how those atoms are arranged. One way to show how an organic molecule is arranged is by using a structural formula. The following is the **structural formula** for one arrangement of C_4H_8.

$$H-\overset{\displaystyle H}{\underset{\displaystyle H}{C}}-\overset{\displaystyle H}{\underset{\displaystyle H}{C}}-\overset{\displaystyle H}{C}=\overset{\displaystyle H}{\underset{\displaystyle H}{C}}-H$$

Structural Formula of C_4H_8

The structural formula is like a two-dimensional picture of the molecule. The letter C represents a carbon atom, and the letter H a hydrogen. The lines connecting the letters represent bonds; single lines are single bonds, and double lines are double bonds.

Hydrocarbons containing only single bonds are called **alkanes.** They include many fuels having the suffix *-ane,* such as methane and butane. The names of alkanes are formed by using various root names that indicate the number of carbon atoms.

Hydrocarbon Prefixes	
Number of Carbon Atoms	Root Word
1	meth-
2	eth-
3	prop-
4	but-
5	pent-
6	hex-
7	hept-
8	oct-
9	non-
10	dec-

10. Organic Chemistry (continued)

Because of the way the hydrogens are added to the carbons, if a molecule has n carbon atoms, it will have $2n + 2$ hydrogen atoms. The general formula expressing the relationship is C_nH_{2n+2}.

Because alkanes have only single bonds, no more hydrogen atoms can be added to them. They are called **saturated hydrocarbons.** Saturated hydrocarbons are filled to capacity with hydrogen atoms. **Unsaturated hydrocarbons** are not filled to capacity. Some alkanes have branched structures, rather than straight molecules.

The atoms of alkane molecules are free to rotate around their bonds. When two structures differ only as a result of rotations around bonds, they are called **conformations** of each other. Other molecules may have the same molecular formula, but different structural formulas. These are called **structural isomers.**

Hydrocarbons containing any double bonds are **alkenes,** and those containing any triple bonds are **alkynes.** Compounds in these groups are named by using the root names used for the alkanes with the suffix *-ene* for alkenes, and *-yne* for alkynes. The general formula for alkenes is C_nH_{2n}, and for alkynes is C_nH_{2n-2}. Thus, two carbons joined by a single bond form the alkane called ethane. Ethene is formed by a double bond, and ethyne by a triple bond.

Hydrocarbons containing rings of carbon are called **cyclic hydrocarbons.** Because a closed chain cannot hold as many hydrogen atoms, the general formula for these molecules is C_nH_{2n}.

Benzene is a cyclic hydrocarbon whose bonds are a hybrid, or combination, of single and double bonds. These hybrid bonds make the benzene ring especially stable. Many compounds built on benzene have distinctive odors, and are known as **aromatic compounds.**

10.3 What are polymers?

Large organic molecules made of small repeating units, or **monomers,** are called **polymers.** Starch and cellulose are polymers containing the simple sugar glucose as a monomer. Many synthetic fabrics and materials, such as polyethylene and nylon, are polymers.

Polymers are synthesized by linking monomers in one of two ways. In the process known as addition polymerization, a double bond in one monomer is broken, and the carbon then bonds with the carbon in another monomer. That, in turn, breaks the double bond in the second monomer, and in a chain reaction, thousands of monomers can be linked. In condensation polymerization, a group of atoms at one end of the monomer reacts with another group at the other end of a second monomer, splitting off water or some other product, and condensing the two monomers into one substance. The same process can take place over and over until a very long polymer is built.

Many synthetic polymers are **biodegradable;** that is, they are broken down to small carbon compounds by natural biological processes. They are recycled into the natural patterns of carbon and other compounds moving through living and nonliving things. Other synthetic polymers are **nonbiodegradable,** and remain in the environment for long periods, in many cases much longer than a human lifetime.

10. Organic Chemistry (continued)

10.4 What kinds of organic compounds are there?

When atoms or groups of atoms are added to hydrocarbons, the resulting compounds are called hydrocarbon derivatives. Although there is a bewildering variety of these derivatives, they can be classified into some major groups by their **functional groups,** which are atoms or groups of atoms that give a molecule a characteristic chemical behavior.

If one or more of the hydrogen atoms of a hydrocarbon is replaced by halogen atoms, the compound is a **halocarbon.** This is symbolized by R—X, where R stands for the hydrocarbon part of the molecule and X is any halogen atom. If a hydrocarbon is replaced by a hydroxyl group, an **alcohol** (R—OH) is formed. If two hydrocarbon chains are attached to the same oxygen atom, the compound is an **ether** (symbolized by R—O—R', where R' stands for a second hydrocarbon chain).

Halocarbons (CFCs, for example) have in the past been used as aerosol propellants, but are now being phased out because they damage the ozone layer in the atmosphere. Alcohols with up to four carbon atoms are polar and water-soluble; they are used as solvents. Ethers have been used as anesthetics and solvents. Small ethers are soluble in water and are polar.

A **carbonyl group** (C=O) at the end of a carbon chain makes up an **aldehyde** (R—CHO). If the carbonyl group is in the middle of the chain, the compound is a **ketone** (R—CO—R'). Adding the suffix -al to one of the hydrocarbon root names indicates that the compound is an aldehyde. Adding the suffix -one shows that it is a ketone.

A **carboxylic acid** (R—COOH) contains a **carboxyl group** (—COOH). Carboxylic acids are named by adding the suffix -oic to the hydrocarbon root name. Many foods contain carboxylic acids. If the H atom of a carboxyl group is replaced by a hydrocarbon chain (R—COOR'), the compound is an **ester.** Esters can be made by reacting a carboxylic acid with an alcohol. They get their names from those sources, having a first name with the alcohol's root name and the suffix -yl, and a last name based on the acid's root name and having the suffix -oate. Esters typically have pleasant, fruity odors. They are sometimes used to make food and household products fragrant. The following chart shows examples of esters and the fragrances associated with them.

Selected Esters and Their Fragrances

Alcohol	Acid	Ester	Fragrance
ethanol	butanoic acid	ethyl butanoate	pineapple
pentanol	ethanoic acid	pentyl ethanoate	banana
octanol	ethanoic acid	octyl ethanoate	orange
methanol	salicylic acid	methyl salicylate	wintergreen
methanol	butanoic acid	methyl butanoate	apple

Amino, or –NH$_2$, groups may be attached to hydrocarbon chains, forming amines (R—NH$_2$); or, if an amino group is attached to the carbon atom of a carbonyl group, the compound is called an amide (R—CONH$_2$). Amines are named by adding the suffix -amine to the root name. Amides are formed by adding the suffix -amide. Amines and amides are both found in biological compounds. **Amino acids** (HOOC—R—NH$_2$) are especially important in organisms. Amino acids have an amino group and a carboxyl group.

10. Organic Chemistry (continued)

10.5 Which organic compounds make up living things?

Biochemistry is the study of chemistry in living organisms. Four major classes of molecules—carbohydrates, lipids, proteins, and nucleic acids—are found in living things.

Two important biochemical processes are photosynthesis and cellular respiration. Carbon dioxide and water are converted to oxygen and glucose by plants during photosynthesis; in the reverse process, plant or animal cells oxidize glucose to carbon dioxide and water during cellular respiration.

The equation for photosynthesis is

$$6\,CO_2 + 6\,H_2O \rightarrow C_6H_{12}O_6 + 6\,O_2$$

During photosynthesis, green plants use the sun's energy to combine carbon dioxide from the air with water from the soil to form glucose, a simple sugar, and oxygen. Energy is stored in the sugar as chemical energy. Animals and plants both use oxygen from the air to oxidize glucose for its stored energy in the reverse reaction, called cellular respiration:

$$C_6H_{12}O_6 + 6\,O_2 \rightarrow 6\,CO_2 + 6\,H_2O$$

Respiration actually occurs gradually in many steps, with the energy being released as needed. A compound known as ATP (adenosine triphosphate) can store energy in its phosphate bonds, and provides energy for some of the steps in respiration, becoming ADP (adenosine diphosphate) in the process. During other steps, ADP is converted back to ATP to be used again.

Carbohydrates, starches and sugars, are made from aldehydes and ketones that contain many hydroxyl groups. The general carbohydrate formula is $C_nH_{2n}O_n$. Some have a straight-chain structure, and others are rings.

Glucose is a simple sugar with the formula $C_6H_{12}O_6$. Glucose is important because of its central role in photosynthesis and cellular respiration. Because it has 6 carbon atoms, it is called a **hexose.** Sugars with 5 carbon atoms are called **pentoses.** Sugars that cannot be broken down into small units are called **monosaccharides;** they can combine chemically to form double sugars, or **disaccharides,** and large polymers, or **polysaccharides.** Monosaccharides can be linked together through a process called **dehydration synthesis.** In this process, a hydrogen atom is removed from one monosaccharide, and a hydroxyl is removed from the other. The hydrogen and hydroxyl are replaced by a new bond that joins the two monosaccharides. The hydrogen and hydroxyl form a water molecule. Conversely, when monosaccharides are formed from larger compounds, it is by **hydrolysis,** or the reverse process of dehydration synthesis. In hydrolysis, bonds between monosaccharides are broken by the addition of water.

Lipids are water-insoluble molecules made of carbon, hydrogen, and oxygen. The major types of lipids are fats, oils, and waxes. Lipids are formed by esterification reactions—combinations of organic acids with alcohols to form esters. If the alcohol is a glycerol, which has three hydroxyl groups, the resulting lipid is a **triglyceride.** Glycerol combines with three long-chain fatty acids in this reaction.

Fats and oils are the two types of triglycerides. In general, fats are solid at room temperature and are made with saturated fatty acids. Oils are liquid at room temperature and are made with unsaturated fatty acids. Oils can be made solid, with the consistency of fats, in a **hydrogenation** process that adds hydrogen atoms to the compounds at the double-bond sites.

Other lipids include the heavy, waterproof substances called waxes, in which the alcohol backbone is not glycerol. **Phospholipids** and **steroids** are also lipids. Phospholipids help make up cell membranes, and steroids form a variety of important compounds that include cholesterol and the sex hormones.

10. Organic Chemistry *(continued)*

Proteins are large amino acid polymers. They are structural materials for the body, and many perform important functions as workers and messengers in the body. While there are only 20 different amino acids, they can be joined in any sequence, making a large variety of protein structures possible. Having a hydrogen at one end and a hydroxyl group at the other, they can be joined in a dehydration synthesis reaction. The bond between adjoining amino acids is called a **peptide bond.**

The sequence of amino acids makes up a protein's **primary structure.** The shape of the protein, such as a helix or pleated sheet, is its **secondary structure.** Finally, the shape of the entire molecule is its **tertiary structure.** That shape can be disrupted by changes in temperature, pH, or other factors that disrupt bonds inside or among molecules. Unfolding of the protein is called **denaturation.** An example of the results of denaturation can be seen in cooked egg white.

Enzymes are the most specialized proteins. They act as catalysts in the body, regulating the speed of reactions. Reactants are brought together by enzymes having specific shapes into which the reactants must fit. Vitamins are less specialized proteins that sometimes act as coenzymes (that is, helper enzymes).

Deoxyribonucleic acid, or DNA, and ribonucleic acid, or RNA, are **nucleic acids.** They are polymers of **nucleotides.** Nucleotides are compounds made up of a five-carbon sugar (ribose), a phosphate group, and a base. The sugars can be joined in long chains, called nucleic acids. The bases in adjacent chains can join also, forming cross-links between molecules. Both DNA and RNA contain the bases adenine, cytosine, and guanine, but their fourth base differs. In DNA the fourth base is thymine; in RNA, it is uracil.

DNA is shaped like a double helix, or corkscrew. It is found in the nuclei of cells and carries the organism's genetic code or hereditary information, and directs the synthesis of protein in cells. A gene is the sequence of DNA nucleotides that makes up the genetic code, or instructions, for synthesizing a protein.

There are three types of RNA. One kind of RNA carries the genetic code from the nucleus to the rest of the cell, where another kind of RNA assembles amino acids in a sequence corresponding to the sequence of bases in DNA. A third kind assists in the assembly of the protein.

10. *Summary of Key Concepts*

At the beginning of Essential 10 you were asked if compounds are exactly the same regardless of whether they are synthesized in a laboratory or in a living organism. Read your statements again, and in the space below add to or change them based on what you have learned in Essential 10. Then review the key concepts below.

_____

_____

_____

10.1 The element carbon can be found in several forms, or allotropes, such as diamond, graphite, and amorphous carbon. Because carbon atoms have a valence shell that is half filled and the bonding electrons are close to the nucleus, the atoms form strong covalent bonds. In addition, they form long, stable chains rather than diatomic molecules. A molecule containing carbon is organic; but oxides of carbon and carbonates are considered inorganic.

10.2 A compound consisting of carbon and hydrogen only is a hydrocarbon. Hydrocarbons are nonpolar molecules that may be straight or branched chains, or rings. Hydrocarbons containing only single bonds are called alkanes. Hydrocarbons containing any double bonds are alkenes, and those containing any triple bonds are alkynes. Benzene, a cyclic hydrocarbon, has bonds that are a hybrid between single and double bonds.

10.3 Large organic molecules made of small repeating units (monomers) and called polymers. Monomers are joined to form polymers through addition polymerization or condensation polymerization. Addition polymerization involves the breaking of double bonds. Condensation polymerization involves splitting off water and joining the ends of monomers.

10.4 When atoms or groups of atoms are added to hydrocarbons, the resulting compounds are called hydrocarbon derivatives. If one or more of the hydrogen atoms of a hydrocarbon is replaced by a halogen atom, the compound is a halocarbon. If the hydrogen is replaced by a hydroxyl group, the compound is an alcohol. If two hydrocarbon chains are attached to the same oxygen atom, the compound is an ether. A carbonyl group ($C=O$) at the end of a carbon chain forms an aldehyde. If the carbonyl group is in the middle of the chain, the compound is a ketone. A carboxylic acid contains a carboxyl group (COOH). If the H atom of a carboxyl group is replaced by a hydrocarbon chain, the compound is an ester. Amino, or $-NH_2$, groups may be attached to hydrocarbon chains, forming amines; or if an amino group is attached to the carbon atom of a carbonyl group, the compound is called an amide.

10.5 Carbon dioxide and water are converted to oxygen and glucose by plants during photosynthesis; in the reverse process, plant or animal cells oxidize food to carbon dioxide and water during cellular respiration. Carbohydrates are made from aldehydes and ketones that contain many hydroxyl groups. Most foods are carbohydrates. Lipids are water-insoluble molecules. Fats, oils, and waxes are lipids. Proteins are amino acid polymers. Many tissues in the body are made of proteins, and so are enzymes that catalyze important reactions in the body. DNA and RNA are polymers of nucleotides called nucleic acids. These molecules store genetic information and assemble proteins based on that information.

10. Summary of Key Concepts (continued)

Key Terms Review

On the line provided, write the term from the list that matches each description.

alcohol   conformations   monomer
alkene   dehydration synthesis   photosynthesis
amine   functional group   structural isomers
carbonyl group   hydrolysis   unsaturated hydrocarbon
cellular respiration   hydroxyl group

_____ 1. compound made entirely of carbon and hydrogen, and that can take on more hydrogen atoms

_____ 2. compounds having the same structural formula, but rotated around single bonds

_____ 3. compounds having the same molecular formula but different structural formulas

_____ 4. hydrocarbon that contains one or more double bonds

_____ 5. single unit that is repeated in a long chain

_____ 6. part of a hydrocarbon derivative that gives the compound characteristic chemical properties

_____ 7. –OH

_____ 8. –COOH

_____ 9. compound containing an –NH$_2$ functional group

_____ 10. compound containing an –OH functional group

_____ 11. formation of glucose by plants

_____ 12. oxidation of glucose in organisms

_____ 13. joining by splitting off a molecule of water

_____ 14. splitting by adding water

10. Summary of Key Concepts (continued)

Assess Your Knowledge

Circle the letter of the answer that best completes the sentence or answers the question.

1. Which is an allotrope of carbon?

    a. benzene

    b. octane

    c. coal

    d. iron ore

2. Which of the following is an organic compound?

    a. C_5H_{12}

    b. N_5H_{12}

    c. CO_2

    d. H_2CO_3

3. An alkene might have the formula

    a. C_5H_5.

    b. C_5H_8.

    c. C_5H_{12}.

    d. C_5H_{10}.

4. Which of the following is not a halocarbon?

    a. R—OCC_{12}

    b. R—OCH_2

    c. C_4HBr_7

    d. C_4F_6

5. The functional group –CHO is found in

    a. ketones.

    b. amines.

    c. aldehydes.

    d. alcohols.

6. Which of the following is an example of a six-carbon sugar?

    a. hexose

    b. pentose

    c. ribose

    d. glucose

10. *Summary of Key Concepts* (continued)

7. An ester can be synthesized from the reaction between an alcohol and a(n)
   a. ketone.
   b. aldehyde.
   c. amide.
   d. carboxylic acid.

8. A steroid is one type of
   a. lipid.
   b. protein.
   c. carbohydrate.
   d. nucleic acid.

9. The unfolding of protein chains is called
   a. dehydration.
   b. esterification.
   c. denaturation.
   d. tertiary structure.

10. Amino acids in proteins are joined by
    a. peptide bonds.
    b. hydrogen bonds.
    c. double bonds.
    d. unsaturated bonds.

Final Assessment

Circle the letter of the answer that best completes the sentence or answers each question.

1. A proton is a particle that has a
   a. mass similar to that of an electron but with an opposite charge.
   b. mass similar to that of a neutron but with the same charge as an electron.
   c. charge opposite to that of an electron and with a mass similar to that of a neutron.
   d. charge equal to that of an electron but with a greater mass.

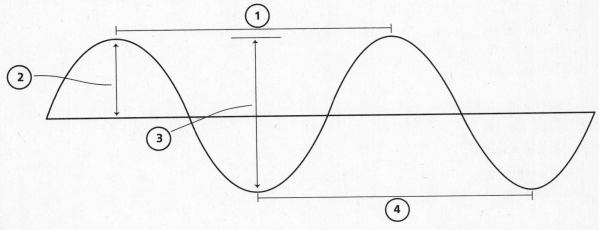

2. Which number in the figure above represents the amplitude of a wave?
   a. 1
   b. 2
   c. 3
   d. 4

3. Which class of organic compounds is made up of large amino acid polymers?
   a. lipids
   b. carbohydrates
   c. proteins
   d. polysaccharides

4. Which of the following statements does not describe a physical property?
   a. The solution is red.
   b. The density of the sample is 3.45 g/mL.
   c. The match is 2.45 cm long.
   d. The match is a solid.

Final Assessment (continued)

5. H_2SO_4, sulfuric acid, is a(n)
   a. carboxylic acid.
   b. binary acid.
   c. oxy acid.
   d. weak acid.

6. Which of the following is not a periodic trend?
   a. energy of activation
   b. atomic radius
   c. onization energy
   d. electron affinity

7. A pH of 6 indicates a
   a. basic solution.
   b. neutral solution.
   c. very acidic solution.
   d. slightly acidic solution.

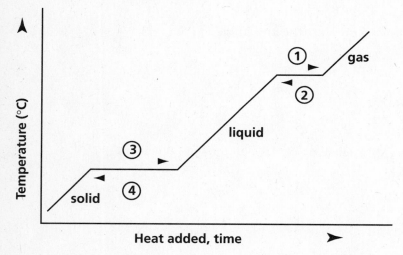

8. On the heating curve diagram above, what number represents the melting of the solid?
   a. 1
   b. 2
   c. 3
   d. 4

Final Assessment (continued)

9. What is the molarity, M, of a solution containing 45. g of sodium hydroxide, NaOH, in 250 mL of water?

   a. 0.18 M

   b. 0.0045 M

   c. 0.45 M

   d. 4.5 M

10. Which of the following is the balanced equation for the reaction between sodium iodide and sulfuric acid?

   a. $4 \, NaI \, (s) + 2 \, H_2SO_4 \, (aq) \rightarrow H_2S \, (g) + 2 \, I_2 \, (s) + 2 \, Na_2SO_4 \, (aq) + 2 \, H_2O \, (l)$

   b. $2 \, NaI \, (s) + H_2SO_4 \, (aq) \rightarrow H_2S \, (g) + I_2 \, (s) + Na_2SO_4 \, (aq) + H_2O \, (l)$

   c. $8 \, NaI \, (s) + 5 \, H_2SO_4 \, (aq) \rightarrow H_2S \, (g) + 4 \, I_2 \, (s) + 4 \, Na_2SO_4 \, (aq) + 4 \, H_2O \, (l)$

   d. $4 \, NaI \, (s) + 2 \, H_2SO_4 \, (aq) \rightarrow H_2S \, (g) + 2 \, I_2 \, (s) + 2 \, Na_2SO_4 \, (aq) + H_2O \, (l)$

11. The equation for the reaction between carbon monoxide and water is

$$CO \, (g) + H_2O \, (g) \rightarrow H_2 \, (g) + CO_2 \, (g)$$

   Which of the following is the equilibrium expression for this reaction?

   a. $K_{eq} = [H_2][CO_2]$

   b. $K_{eq} = [CO][H_2O]$

   c. $K_{eq} = \dfrac{[CO][H_2O]}{[H_2][CO_2]}$

   d. $K_{eq} = \dfrac{[HO][CO_2]}{[CO][H_2O]}$

12. Which type of reaction is illustrated by the equation $CaCO_3 \rightarrow CaO + CO_2$?

   a. decomposition reaction

   b. combustion reaction

   c. single replacement reaction

   d. direct combination reaction

Final Assessment (continued)

13. Which substance is the reducing agent in the reaction shown by the following equation?

$$2\ Fe_2O_3 + 3\ C \rightarrow 4\ Fe + 3\ CO_2$$

   a. Fe
   b. CO_2
   c. Fe_2O_3
   d. C

14. The structural formula for hexane is
   a. CH_3–CH_2–CH_2–CH_2–CH_2–CH_2–CH_3.
   b. CH_3–CH_2–CH_2–CH_2–CH_2–CH_3.
   c. CH_2–CH_2–CH_2–CH_2–CH_2–CH=CH_2.
   d. CH_2–CH_2–CH_2–CH_2–CH_2–CH_2–CH_3.

15. One mole of iron(III) chloride, $FeCl_3$, has a mass of
   a. 91.3 g.
   b. 202.9 g.
   c. 126.8 g.
   d. 162.3 g.

16. What is the empirical formula for a compound containing 25.9% nitrogen and 74.1% oxygen?
   a. $N_{25.9}O_{74.1}$
   b. N_2O_5
   c. NO_3
   d. NO_2

17. If a gas occupies 45.6 L at 250 K, what volume does it occupy if the temperature changes to 300 K? Assume constant pressure.
   a. 54.7 L
   b. 2280 L
   c. 91.2 L
   d. 38.0 L

Final Assessment (continued)

18. Standard temperature and pressure (STP) is defined as
    a. 0°C (273 K) and 1 atm.
    b. 20°C (293 K) and 1 atm.
    c. 25°C (298 K) and 1 atm.
    d. 27°C (300 K) and 1 atm.

19. In an oxidation-reduction reaction, the substance that loses one or more electrons
    a. is oxidized.
    b. is reduced.
    c. reverts to its elemental state.
    d. becomes negatively charged.

20. If the Gibbs free energy (ΔG) of a reaction is negative, the reaction is said to be
    a. at equilibrium.
    b. spontaneous.
    c. endothermic.
    d. exothermic.

21. If the half-life of a radioactive isotope is 100 years, how many years does it take for only one-eighth of a certain sample of it to be left?
    a. 200 years
    b. 300 years
    c. 400 years
    d. 800 years

22. Which of the following reactions produces energy in the sun?
    a. nuclear fission reaction
    b. nuclear chain reaction
    c. nuclear fusion reaction
    d. nuclear plasma reaction

Final Assessment (continued)

23. The functional group of a carboxylic acid is represented by the general formula
    a. R–X.
    b. R–OH.
    c. R–CO–R'.
    d. R–COOH.

24. The elements in Column 2 of the periodic table are called the
    a. alkaline earth metals.
    b. alkali metals.
    c. halogens.
    d. noble gases.

25. Which of the following is not a colligative property of a solution?
    a. vapor pressure reduction
    b. boiling point elevation
    c. solubility
    d. freezing point depression

Math Refresher

Throughout your study of chemistry, you will need to solve a number of math problems. This Math Refresher is designed to help you review those mathematical topics that you may find challenging. You may wish to study this material before working on problems presented in the textbook.

Equations and Formulas

An equation is a mathematical sentence that contains a variable and an equal sign. An equation expresses a relationship between two or more quantities. A formula is a special kind of equation. A formula shows relationships between quantities that are always true. To solve for a quantity in an equation or formula, substitute the known values. Be sure to include units.

Example

Find the mass of a sample of aluminum with a volume of 5 cm³ and a density of 2.7 g/cm³.

$$\text{density} = \text{mass/volume}$$

$$2.7 \text{ g/cm}^3 = \frac{\text{mass}}{5 \text{ cm}^3}$$

$$5 \text{ cm}^3 \times 2.7 \text{ g/cm}^3 = \text{mass}$$

$$13.5 \text{ g} = \text{mass}$$

Exponents

A base is a number that is used as a factor. An exponent is a number that tells how many times the base is to be used as a factor. A power is a number that can be expressed as a product in which all of the factors are the same.

Example

$$2 \times 2 \times 2 \times 2 \times 2 = 32$$
$$2^5 = 32$$

Some special cases exist with exponents. Any number is raised to the zero power is always 1. For example, 5^0 is 1 and 6^0 is 1. Any number raised to the first power is that number. For example, 5^1 is 5 and 6^1 is 6. The only exception to that rule is the number 0, which is always zero regardless of the power it is raised to.

MULTIPLICATION

When adding and subtracting exponents, like terms are added together. When exponents are multiplied, they are handled differently. Multiplication of exponents can be expressed in three different ways.

To multiply together exponents with the same base, add the exponents. The general expression for multiplying exponents with the same base is $x^a \times x^b = x^{a+b}$.

Example
$$3^2 \times 3^4 = (3 \times 3) \times (3 \times 3 \times 3 \times 3)$$
$$= 3^6 = 729$$

To raise a power to a power, keep the base and multiply the exponents. The general expression is $(x^a)^b = x^{ab}$.

Example
$$(3^2)^3 = (3^2) \times (3^2) \times (3^2) = 3^6 = 729$$

To raise a product to a power, raise each factor to the power. The general expression is $(xy)^n = x^n y^n$.

Example
$$(3 \times 9)^2 = 3^2 \times 9^2 = 9 \times 81 = 729$$

DIVISION

To divide exponents by other exponents with the same base, keep the base and subtract the exponents. The general expression is
$$\frac{x^a}{x^b} = x^{a-b}.$$

Example
$$\frac{5^6}{5^4} = 5^2 = 25$$

To raise a quotient to a power, raise the numerator and denominator to the power. The general expression is
$$\left(\frac{x}{y}\right)^n = \frac{x^n}{y^n}.$$

Example
$$\left(\frac{4}{5}\right)^2 = \frac{4^2}{5^2} = \frac{16}{25}$$

When the exponent of the denominator is greater than the exponent of the numerator, the

Math Refresher (continued)

exponent is negative. A negative exponent follows the general expression $x^{-n} = \frac{1}{x^n}$.

Example

$$2^3 \div 2^5 = 2^{3-5} = 2^{-2} = \frac{1}{2^9} = \frac{1}{4}$$

Fractions

ADDITION AND SUBTRACTION

To add or subtract fractions that have the same denominator, add or subtract the numerators, then write the sum or difference over the denominator. Express the answer in lowest terms.

Examples

$$\frac{3}{10} + \frac{1}{10} = \frac{3+1}{10} = \frac{4}{10} = \frac{2}{5}$$

$$\frac{5}{7} - \frac{2}{7} = \frac{5-2}{7} = \frac{3}{7}$$

To add or subtract fractions with different denominators, find the least common denominator. Write an equivalent fraction for each fraction using the least common denominator. Then add or subtract the numerators. Write the sum or difference over the least common denominator and express the answer in lowest terms.

Examples

$$\frac{1}{3} + \frac{3}{5} = \frac{5}{15} + \frac{9}{15} = \frac{5+9}{15} = \frac{14}{15}$$

$$\frac{7}{8} - \frac{1}{4} = \frac{7}{8} - \frac{2}{8} = \frac{7-2}{8} = \frac{5}{8}$$

MULTIPLICATION

To multiply two or more fractions, multiply the numerators to obtain the numerator of the product. Then multiply the denominators to obtain the denominator of the product. Whenever possible, divide any numerator or denominator by their greatest common factor before multiplying. Express the answer in lowest terms.

Examples

$$\frac{3}{5} \times \frac{2}{7} = \frac{3 \times 2}{5 \times 7} = \frac{6}{35}$$

$$\frac{4}{14} \times \frac{6}{9} = \frac{2 \times 2}{7 \times 2} = \frac{2 \times 3}{3 \times 3} = \frac{2 \times 2}{7 \times 3} = \frac{4}{21}$$

DIVISION

To divide one fraction by another, invert the divisor and multiply the two fractions. Express the answer in lowest terms.

Examples

$$\frac{2}{5} \div \frac{3}{4} = \frac{2}{5} \times \frac{4}{3} = \frac{2 \times 4}{5 \times 3} = \frac{8}{15}$$

$$\frac{9}{16} \div \frac{5}{8} = \frac{9}{16} \times \frac{8}{5} = \frac{9 \times 1}{2 \times 5} = \frac{9}{10}$$

Graphing

Graphs are useful for presenting the results of a scientific experiment so that the results are clearer and easier to understand. Graphs can be line graphs, bar graphs, pie graphs, or other types. The type of graph that is best depends on the type of data you are trying to present with it. You will probably use line graphs most often to represent data from your experiments.

Graphing is most convenient when the form of a graph is a straight line. For example, suppose you have twenty small balls that each has a mass of 10 grams. Each time you add one ball to a container, the total mass increases by 10 grams. If you plot the number of balls on the x-axis and the total mass on the y-axis, the result will be a straight-line graph. The total mass increases 10 times as fast as the number of balls.

You plot the data by drawing a point on the intercept identified by the x and y values. For example, the total mass of the balls after you add the fourth ball is 40 grams. The intercept that identifies these values is (4 balls, 40 grams) or simply (4, 40). Count over to 4 on the x-axis and straight up to 40 on the y-axis. Repeat this procedure for all your data.

Math Refresher (continued)

The equation for a straight line can be described as

$$y = mx + b$$

Where m is the slope of the line and b is the point at which the line intersects the y-axis when the value on the x-axis is set to zero. The function $y = 2x + 4$ is plotted below.

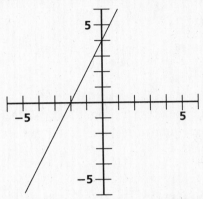

For this graph, the slope is 2 and the line intersects the y-axis at 4. In this example, the value of the y intercept increases twice as quickly as that of the x intercept.

Other data may result in graphs that are not straight lines. For these, you plot the data in the same way. However, you cannot predict additional intercepts on the graph by using the equation for a line.

Slope of a Line

The slope of a line is the ratio of the change in vertical distance to the change in horizontal distance. In general, the slope of a line, m, that passes through two points (x_1, y_1) and (x_2, y_2) is the ratio of the difference of the y-values of these points to the difference of the corresponding x-values. The slope, m, is also found in the equation of a line $y = mx + b$.

$$\text{Slope of line} = \frac{\text{difference in y-values}}{\text{difference in x-values}}$$

$$m = \frac{y_2 - y_1}{x_2 - x_1}$$

Example

If two points on a line are (4, 40), and (6, 60), what is the slope of the line?

$$m = \frac{y_2 - y_1}{x_2 - x_1}$$

$$= \frac{60 - 40}{6 - 4}$$

$$= \frac{20}{2}$$

$$= 10$$

Logarithms

A logarithm is the exponent to which a number or base must be raised to produce a given number. The function $x = 10^y$ is the inverse of the function $\log x = y$. Here x is the number and y is the logarithm of x to the base 10. Base 10 logarithms are called common logarithms.

Example

$$\log 10^2 = 2$$

Logarithms are useful when comparing numbers that have a large magnitude of difference.

Logarithms can be solved with a scientific calculator. On scientific calculators, the key for the common logarithm is marked [log]. To find the common logarithm of a number, enter that number and press the [log] key. The log will be displayed in the screen. Logs are generally written with four digits to the right of the decimal.

Example

Find the log of 567.

Enter 567.

Press [log].

The display reads 2.7535831.

$$\log 567 = 2.7536$$

The antilog is the number that results from raising the base of the logarithm to the power of the logarithm. To find the antilog of a logarithm on most calculators, enter the log number, press

Math Refresher (continued)

the [inverse] key, and then press the [log] key. This will display the number to within the accuracy of the calculator.

Example
Enter 2.7536.
Press [inv] and then press [log].
The display reads 567.02212.

Percents and Decimals

To convert a percent to a decimal, write the number without the percent sign and move the decimal point two places to the left. Add a zero before the decimal.

Examples
38% = 0.38
74% = 0.74
13.92% = 0.1392

When you know a decimal value of 100, you can convert the decimal to a percent by moving the decimal point two places to the right and adding the percent sign.

Examples
0.12 = 12%
0.46 = 46%
0.8215 = 82.15%

Ratios and Proportions

A ratio compares two numbers or quantities. A ratio is often written as a fraction in which the number being compared is the numerator and the number to which it is being compared is the denominator. The fraction is then expressed in lowest terms. A ratio may also be written with a colon.

Examples
Ratio of 3 to 4
3 to 4, or $\frac{3}{4}$, or $3:4$

Ration of 10 to 5
10 to 5, or $\frac{10}{5} = \frac{2}{1}$, or $2:1$

A proportion is a mathematical sentence that states that two ratios are equivalent. To write a proportion, place an equal sign between the two equivalent ratios.

Examples
The ratio of 6 to 9 is the same as the ratio of 8 to 12.

$$\frac{6}{9} = \frac{8}{12}$$

The ratio of 2 to 4 is the same as the ratio of 7 to 14.

$$\frac{2}{4} = \frac{7}{14}$$

You can set up a proportion to determine an unknown quantity. Use X to represent the unknown.

Examples
What number has the same ratio to 15 as 3 has to 9?

$$\frac{3}{9} = \frac{X}{15}$$

Two out of five students have blue notebooks. If the same ratio of blue textbooks to students exists in a class of twenty students, how many students have blue notebooks?

$$\frac{2}{5} = \frac{X}{20}$$

To find the value of the unknown number in a proportion, cross-multiply and then divide both sides of the equation by the number that comes before X.

Examples

$$\frac{3}{9} \Join \frac{X}{15} \qquad \frac{2}{5} \Join \frac{X}{20}$$

$$3 \times 15 = 9 \times X \qquad 2 \times 20 = 5 \times X$$

$$45 = 9X \qquad 40 = 5X$$

$$5 = X \qquad 8 = X$$

Rounding

The results of calculations that have more digits than needed number of significant digits must be rounded off. Rounding numbers is

Math Refresher (continued)

performed using the following rule. If the first digit after the last significant digit is less than 5, round down. If the first digit after the last significant digit is 5 or more, round up.

Example

1577 rounded to three significant digits is 1580.

1574 rounded to three significant digits is 1570.

2.456862 rounded to three significant digits is 2.46.

2.456862 rounded to four significant digits is 2.457.

Scientfic Notation

You have learned that scientific notation is used to express a very large number or a very small number. To express a number that is greater than 1, you can group the powers of 10 together. One method of determining the correct scientific notation for large numbers is to move the decimal point to the left until it is located to the right of the first nonzero number. The number of places that you move the decimal becomes the positive exponent of 10 in the notation.

Examples

2,500,000 can be expressed as

$2.5 \times 10^6 = 2.5 \times 10 \times 10 \times 10 \times 10 \times 10 \times 10$

18,930,000 can be expressed as

$1.893 \times 10^7 = 1.893 \times 10 \times 10 \times 10 \times 10 \times 10 \times 10 \times 10$

To express a number smaller than 1 in scientific notation, move the decimal point to the right until it is located to the right of the first nonzero number. Count the number of places that you move the decimal point and write this number as the negative exponent of 10.

Examples

0.000056 can be written as 5.6×10^{-5}

$$= \frac{5.6}{10 \times 10 \times 10 \times 10 \times 10}$$

0.0027 can be written as 2.7×10^{-3}

$$= \frac{2.7}{10 \times 10 \times 10}$$

To add or subtract numbers written in scientific notation, the exponents of the numbers must be the same. If they are different, you must rewrite one of the numbers to make them the same. Then rewrite the answer so that only one number is to the left of the decimal point.

Examples

Add 3.2×10^3 and 5.1×10^2.

$$\begin{array}{r} 32 \times 10^2 \\ + 5.1 \times 10^2 \\ \hline 37.1 \times 10^2 \rightarrow 3.71 \times 10^3 \end{array}$$

Subtract 5.4×10^7 from 6.8×10^8.

$$\begin{array}{r} 68 \times 10^7 \\ - 5.4 \times 10^7 \\ \hline 62.6 \times 10^7 \rightarrow 6.26 \times 10^8 \end{array}$$

To multiply or divide numbers in scientific notation, the exponents must be added or subtracted.

Examples

Find the product of 1.2×10^3 and 3.4×10^4.

$$(1.2 \times 10^3)(3.4 \times 10^4) = (4.08 \times 10^{3+4})$$
$$= 4.08 \times 10^7$$

Divide 5.0×10^9 by 2.5×10^6.

$$(5.0 \times 10^9) \div (2.5 \times 10^6) = (2.0 \times 10^{9-6})$$
$$= 2.0 \times 10^3$$

Math Refresher (continued)

Significant Digits

Chemistry involves working with many measurements that are not exact. When inexact measurements are combined in calculations, the uncertainty of each measurement must be correctly reflected in the final result. Your final answer should only be as accurate as the quantities you used in calculating that answer. The digits that are accurate or reliable in the answer are called significant digits.

When using significant digits in calculations, you should keep the following three points in mind.

- When an exact number appears in a calculation, it does not affect the number of significant digits in the final answer.
- In multiplication and division, the measurement with the smallest number of significant digits determines how many digits are allowed in the final answer.

Example

$$\text{density} = \frac{\text{mass}}{\text{volume}}$$

$$= 20.79 \text{ g}/5.5 \text{ mL}$$

$$= 3.78 \text{ g/mL}$$

$$= 3.8 \text{ g/mL}$$

The final answer has two significant digits because your answer cannot be more precise than your least precise measurement (5.5 mL).

- In addition and subtraction, the number of significant digits allowed depends on the number with the largest uncertainty.

Example

$$\begin{array}{r} 25.34 \text{ g} \\ 151 \text{ g} \\ + \ 4.009 \text{ g} \\ \hline 180. \text{ g} \end{array}$$

The different measurements have different uncertainties. The measurement with the largest uncertainty is 151 g and it is measured to the nearest gram. Therefore, the answer is reported to the nearest gram. Notice that the decimal point is included to show that the zero is one of the significant digits.

Square Roots and Cube Roots

Finding the root of a number is the inverse operation of raising a number to a power. The square of a number is that number raised to the power of two. The square root of a number is a number to be raised to the power of 2. For example, the square root of 25 is 5, and the square of 5 is 25. Just as a number can be raised to any power, you can take any root of a number. The cube of a number is that number to the power of 3. The cube root is the number to be raised to the power of 3. For example, $2 \times 2 \times 2 = 8$, and so $\sqrt[3]{8} = 2$.

To find a root, find the factor that has been multiplied a number of times to produce a given value. The number of times, n, that the factor has been multiplied is the nth root.

Examples

$$\sqrt{64} = 8$$
$$64 = 8 \times 8$$

$$\sqrt[3]{64} = 4$$
$$64 = 4 \times 4 \times 4$$

Math Refresher (continued)

Dimensional Analysis

Most chemistry problems involve converting measurements from one unit to another. This process is known as dimensional analysis.

You can convert units by using a unit equality. A unit equality is an equation that shows how units are related. The unit equality for converting inches to centimeters is

$$1 \text{ in.} = 2.54 \text{ cm}$$

In other words, 1 inch is just slightly more than 2.5 centimeters.

The next step is to use the unit equality to write a conversion factor. To do this, divide both sides of the unit equality by one of the units. A conversion factor is a ratio that will always be equal to 1.

$$\frac{1 \text{ in.}}{1 \text{ in.}} = \frac{2.54 \text{ cm}}{1 \text{ in.}}$$

$$1 = \frac{2.54 \text{ cm}}{1 \text{ in.}}$$

Dividing both sides of the unit equality by the other unit creates the second conversion factor.

$$\frac{1 \text{ in.}}{2.54 \text{ cm}} = \frac{2.54 \text{ cm}}{2.54 \text{ cm}}$$

$$\frac{1 \text{ in.}}{2.54 \text{ cm}} = 1$$

One of the conversion factors will convert inches to centimeters and the other will convert centimeters to inches. Choose the conversion factor that cancels out the unit that you have a measurement for and leaves the unit that is needed in the answer. Then multiply by that conversion factor.

Example

Convert 25 inches to centimeters. Use *d* to represent the unknown number of centimeters.

$$d = 25 \text{ in.} \times \frac{2.54 \text{ cm}}{1 \text{ in.}}$$

$$= 64 \text{ cm}$$

Sometimes the unit conversions are complicated and require multiple steps to make the complete unit conversion. Sometimes you may not have a conversion factor to convert from the units that you have to the units you desire. You may, however, have conversion factors for intermediate units. In that case, it is usually easiest to group the conversions together into one equation.

Example

Convert 31 meters to millimeters. Use *d* to represent the unknown number of millimeters.

$$d = 31 \text{ m} \times \frac{100 \text{ cm}}{1 \text{ cm}} \times \frac{10 \text{ cm}}{1 \text{ cm}}$$

$$= 31,000 \text{ mm}$$

Math Refresher: Sample and Practice Problems

Acidic Solution or Basic Solution

You are given two aqueous solutions. One solution has an $[OH^-]$ of 1.4×10^{-6} M. The second solution has an $[H_3O^+]$ that is 10 times greater than its OH^- concentration. Calculate the $[H_3O^+]$ for each solution and determine whether each is acidic or basic.

Analyze   The concentration of OH^- ions for the first solution is given. For the second solution, the relative concentrations of OH^- and H_3O^+ ions are given.

Plan   To solve each of these problems, use the definition of K_w. Whichever is greater, $[H_3O^+]$ or $[OH^-]$, determines the acidity or basicity of the solution.

Solve   1. The first solution has an $[OH^-]$ of 1.4×10^{-6} M.

$$[H_3O^+]\,[OH^-] = K_w$$
$$[H_3O^+]\,[1.4 \times 10^{-6}] = 1.0 \times 10^{-14}$$
$$[H_3O^+] = \frac{1.0 \times 10^{-14}}{1.4 \times 10^{-6}}$$
$$[H_3O^+] = 7.1 \times 10^{-9}\ \text{M}$$

The solution is basic.

2. The second solution has an H_3O^+ concentration that is 10 times greater than the OH^- concentration.

Let $[OH^-] = x$ and $[H_3O^+] = 10x$

$$[H_3O^+]\,[OH^-] = K_w$$
$$[x]\,[10x] = 1.0 \times 10^{-14}$$
$$10x^2 = 1.0 \times 10^{-14}$$
$$x^2 = 1.0 \times 10^{-15}$$
$$x = \sqrt{1.0 \times 10^{-15}} = 3.2 \times 10^{-8}$$

So $[OH^-] = 3.2 \times 10^{-8}$ M and $[H_3O^+] = 10 \times (3.2 \times 10^{-8}\ \text{M}) = 3.2 \times 10^{-7}$ M

The solution is slightly acidic.

Evaluate   The concentration of ions can be used to determine whether a solution is acid or basic. If the concentration of OH^- is greater than that of H_3O^+, the solution is basic. If the concentration of H_3O^+ ions is greater than that of OH^- ions, the solution is acidic.

PRACTICE PROBLEMS

1. What is the $[H_3O^+]$ of an aqueous solution with an $[OH^-]$ of 2.3×10^{-9} M? Is the solution acidic or basic? (*Answer*: $[H_3O^+] = 4.3 \times 10^{-6}$ M; *The solution is acidic.*)

2. The OH^- concentration of a solution is 3 times greater than its H_3O^+ concentration. What are the $[OH^-]$ and $[H_3O^+]$? Is the solution acidic or basic? (*Answer*: $[H_3O^+] = 5.7 \times 10^{-8}$ M *and* $[OH^-] = 1.7 \times 10^{-7}$ M; *The solution is basic.*)

Math Refresher: Sample and Practice Problems

Calorimetry

A solution with 25.0 ml of water containing 0.025 mol HCl and a second solution with 25 mL of water containing 0.025 mol NaOH are mixed in a calorimeter. At the start of the reaction, both solutions are 25.0°C. During the reaction, the highest temperature observed is 32.0°C. Calculate the heat released during the reaction. Assume the density of each solution is 1.00 g/mL.

Analyze   You must use the calorimetry data to calculate the ΔH.

Plan   The equation for calculating ΔH is

$$\Delta H = m \times C \times (T_f - T_i)$$

where m is mass, C is specific heat, T_i is initial temperature, and T_f is final temperature.

Solve   Substitute the values into the equation. Use the density of the solutions to calculate the grams of solution.

$$\Delta H = m \times C \times (T_f - T_i)$$
$$= (50.0 \; \cancel{mL} \times 1.00 \; g/\cancel{mL}) \times 4.18 \; J/g°C \times (32.0°C - 25.0°C)$$
$$= 50.0 \; \cancel{g} \times 4.18 \; J/\cancel{g}°\cancel{C} \times 7.0°\cancel{C}$$
$$= 1463 \; J = 1.46 \; kJ$$

Evaluate   The minus sign tells you that heat was released when the HCl and NaOH reacted.

Practice Problems

1. A peanut is burned in a calorimeter. The mass of the peanut is 0.887 g. The calorimeter was filled with 2500 g of water. The initial temperature of the water was 25.0°C and the final temperature of the water was 27.0 °C. What is the change in energy content of the peanut? (*Answer: 20.9 kJ*)

2. A 20.0 g sample of iron was heated to 95.0°C. It was then placed in 100.0 g of water at a temperature of 25°C. What is the resulting temperature of the water in the calorimeter? Assume $\Delta H_{iron} = 0.45 \; J/g°C$; $\Delta H_{water} = 4.18 \; J/g°C$. (*Answer: 26.5°C*)

Math Refresher: Sample and Practice Problems

Charles's Law

What will be the volume of a gas sample at 100.°C if its volume at 35°C is 33.8 L? Assume the pressure of the gas remains unchanged.

Analyze   This problem can be solved using Charles's law. Volume and temperature are variable and the amount of gas and its pressure remain constant.

Plan   Charles's law mathematically states $V_1 T_2 = V_2 T_1$. The amounts for T_1 and V_1 are given. T_1 is the temperature to which the gas is being increased. V_1 is the unknown that must be solved for. Rearrange the equation to solve for V_2. Remember to convert the temperatures for T_1 and T_2 to kelvins.

Solve   Convert the temperature to kelvins. Then substitute into the rearranged equation for Charles's law.

$$T_1(K) = 35°C + 273 = 308\ K$$

$$T_2(K) = 100.°C + 273 = 373\ K$$

$$V_1 T_2 = V_2 T_1$$

$$V_2 = \frac{V_1 T_2}{T_1} = \frac{(33.8\ L)\ (373\ K)}{(308\ K)}$$

$$= 40.9\ L$$

Evaluate   The answer makes sense because as the temperature increases, the volume increases.

PRACTICE PROBLEMS

1. At what temperature will a gas occupy 200 L if it occupies 100 L at 25°C? Assume the pressure of the gas remains unchanged. (*Answer: 596 K*)

2. If a gas occupies 36.5 L at 25°C, what will the volume be if the temperature is dropped to 15°C? Assume the pressure of the gas remains unchanged. (*Answer: 31.6 L*)

Math Refresher: Sample and Practice Problems

Dimensional Analysis

How many centimeters are in 1.60 yards?

Analyze   You are asked to convert yards to centimeters. You do not know a unit equality between yards and centimeters. However, you know that there are unit equalities to convert yards to feet, feet to inches, and inches to centimeters.

Plan   Here are the unit equalities you will need.

$$1 \text{ yard} = 3 \text{ ft}$$
$$1 \text{ ft} = 12 \text{ in.}$$
$$1 \text{ in.} = 2.54 \text{ cm}$$

The conversion factors you can use are

$$\frac{1 \text{ yard}}{3 \text{ft}} = \frac{3 \text{ ft}}{1 \text{ yard}}$$

$$\frac{1 \text{ ft}}{12 \text{ in.}} = \frac{12 \text{ in.}}{1 \text{ ft}}$$

$$\frac{1 \text{ in.}}{2.54 \text{ cm}} = \frac{2.54 \text{ cm}}{1 \text{ in.}}$$

Choose the correct conversion factors by dimensional analyses. The symbol d can be used for the unknown number of centimeters.

Solve

$$d = 1.60 \text{ yards} \times \frac{3 \text{ ft}}{1 \text{ yard}} \times \frac{12 \text{ in.}}{1 \text{ ft}} \times \frac{2.54 \text{ cm}}{1 \text{ in.}}$$

$$d = 146 \text{ cm}$$

Evaluate   The unwanted units canceled from the equation as required, leaving only the units of centimeters. Since 1 yard is almost 100 centimeters, it makes sense that 1.60 yards is almost 150 centimeters.

PRACTICE PROBLEMS

1. How many meters are in 100. yards (100 cm = 1 m)? *(Answer: 91.4 m)*

2. How many inches is 78.8 millimeters (10 mm = 1 cm)? *(Answer 3.10 m)*

Math Refresher: Sample and Practice Problems

Equilibrium Expressions

What is the equilibrium expression for this reaction?

$$4\,NH_3\,(g) + 5\,O_2\,(g) \rightleftharpoons 4\,NO\,(g) + 6\,H_2O\,(g)$$

Analyze You are asked to find the equilibrium expression for a reversible reaction.

Plan The equilibrium expression is the ratio of the product concentrations to the reactant concentrations.

Solve The solubility product expression is

$$K_{eq} = \frac{[NO]^4\,[H_2O]^6}{[NH_3]^4\,[O_2]^5}$$

Evaluate The answer shows the concentrations of the products in the numerator and the concentration of the reactants in the denominator. The concentration of carbon is essentially a constant and does not appear in the answer.

PRACTICE PROBLEMS

1. What is the equilibrium expression for this reaction? (*Answer:* $K_{eq} = \frac{[H_2]^2\,[S_2]}{[H_2S]^2}$)

    $$2\,H_2S \rightleftharpoons 2\,H_2 + S_2$$

2. What is the equilibrium expression for this reaction? (*Answer:* $K_{eq} = \frac{[PCl_3]\,[Cl_2]}{[PCl_5]}$)

    $$PCl_5 \rightleftharpoons PCl_3 + Cl_2$$

Math Refresher: Sample and Practice Problems

Freezing Point Depression

What is the freezing point depression when 25.5 g of glucose ($C_6H_{12}O_6$) is dissolved in 350 g of acetic acid? For acetic acid, K_f is 3.90 C°/m.

Analyze You are given the mass of the solute and solvent and are asked to find the freezing point depression.

Plan The freezing point depression can be calculated from the molal freezing point depression constant and the molality of the solute. You must use the molar mass to find the molality.

Solve Calculate the molality of the solution, making sure to convert from mass to moles.

$$\text{molality} = \frac{\text{mol solute}}{\text{kg solvent}}$$

$$= \frac{25.5 \text{ g } C_6H_{12}O_6}{0.350 \text{ kg solvent}} \times \frac{1 \text{ mol } C_6H_{12}O_6}{180 \text{ g } C_6H_{12}O_6}$$

$$= 0.405 \text{ mol/kg}$$

$$= 0.405 \text{ } m$$

Determine $\Delta T_f = K_f m$.

$$\Delta T_f = 3.90 \text{ C°/m} \times 0.405 \text{ } m$$

$$= 1.58 \text{ C°}$$

Evaluate The answer makes sense because the addition of glucose lowers the freezing point by 1.58 C°.

PRACTICE PROBLEMS

1. What is the freezing point depression when 28.9 g of sucrose ($C_{12}H_{22}O_{11}$) is dissolved in 1500 g of acetic acid? K_f for acetic acid is 3.90 C°/m. (*Answer: 0.220 C°*)

2. What is the freezing point depression when 200 g of glucose ($C_6H_{12}O_6$) is dissolved in 4200 g of water? K_f of water is 1.86 C°/m. (*Answer: 0.492 C°*)

Math Refresher: Sample and Practice Problems

Ideal Gas Law

What is the volume occupied by 15.6 g of butane (C_4H_{10}) at STP?

Analyze   This is a problem for the ideal gas equation, which can be rearranged to solve for V, the volume of gas. Values for the number of moles, temperature, and pressure are provided.

Plan   Rearrange the ideal gas equation to solve for the volume:

$$PV = nRT$$

$$V = \frac{nRT}{P}$$

The temperature must be converted from degrees Celsius to kelvins.

Solve   Convert the temperature to kelvins and the mass of the gas to moles. Then substitute into the rearranged equation above. The value for R is $0.0821 \frac{atm\text{-}L}{mol\text{-}K}$.

$$T(K) = 25°C + 273 = 298 \text{ K}$$

$$n = 15.6 \text{ g } C_4H_{10} \times \frac{1 \text{ mol}}{58 \text{ g } C_4H_{10}}$$

$$= 0.270 \text{ mol}$$

$$V = \frac{nRT}{P}$$

$$= (0.270 \text{ mol}) \, (0.0821 \frac{atm\text{-}L}{mol\text{-}K}) \, \frac{(298 \text{ K})}{(1 \text{ atm})}$$

$$= 6.61 \text{ L}$$

Evaluate   All the units cancel to give the answer in the correct units of volume.

PRACTICE PROBLEMS

1. What is the number of moles of an ideal gas that occupies 63.5 L at 2.20 atm and 100°C? *(Answer: 4.56 mol)*

2. What is the pressure in atmospheres of 25.9 g of chlorine gas in a 750 mL container at 35°C? *(Answer: 14.9 mol)*

Math Refresher: Sample and Practice Problems

Molarity

What is the molarity (M) of a solution formed by mixing 12.6 g of KOH with enough water to make 250 mL of solution?

Analyze   You are given the mass of the solute and the volume of the solution. You are asked to calculate the molarity of the solution.

Plan   To calculate the molarity, you need to convert the mass of the solute to moles using molar mass and the volume of the solution to liters. The resulting information can be used in the molarity equation.

Solve
$$\text{molarity} = \frac{\text{mol solute}}{\text{L solution}}$$

$$= \frac{12.6 \text{ g } \cancel{KOH}}{0.250 \text{ L solution}} \times \frac{1 \text{ mol KOH}}{56.1 \text{ g } \cancel{KOH}}$$

$$= 0.900 \text{ mol/L}$$

$$= 0.900 \text{ M}$$

Evaluate   The units of the answer make sense because the answer describes the concentration of the solution in terms of moles per liter of solution.

PRACTICE PROBLEMS

1. What is the molarity of a solution formed by mixing 100. g of HCl with enough water to make 500 mL of solution? (*Answer: 5.48 M*)

2. What is the molarity of a solution formed by mixing 28 g of NaOH with enough water to make 1.25 L of solution? (*Answer: 0.560 M*)

Math Refresher: Sample and Practice Problems

Percent Yield

A solution containing 3.5 g of KI is mixed with a solution containing excess $Pb(NO_3)_2$. A precipitate of PbI_2 forms. The mass of the precipitate is 3.79 g when dried and weighed. What is the percent yield for this reaction?

Analyze   You are given the mass of the product and are asked to compare the actual mass with the expected mass.

Plan   The expected mass is determined from a stoichiometry, or mass-mass problem. First find the expected mass and then compare it with the actual mass as given in the problem.

Solve   The balanced equation is

$$2 \text{ KI} + Pb(NO_3)_2 \rightarrow PbI_2 + 2 \text{ KNO}_3$$

$$3.5 \text{ g KI} \times \frac{1 \text{ mol KI}}{166 \text{ g KI}} \times \frac{1 \text{ mol PbI}_2}{2 \text{ mol KI}} \times \frac{461 \text{ g PbI}_2}{1 \text{ mol PbI}_2} = 4.86 \text{ g PbI}_2$$

The expected yield is 4.86 g PbI_2.

$$\text{percent yield} = \frac{\text{actual yield}}{\text{expected yield}} \times 100\%$$

$$= \frac{3.79 \text{ g PbI}_2}{4.86 \text{ g PbI}_2} \times 100\%$$

$$= 78.0\%$$

Evaluate   The mass of PbI_2 actually produced is less than the calculated mass. Therefore, the percent yield is less than 100 percent. So the answer is reasonable.

PRACTICE PROBLEMS

1. Acetylene (C_2H_2) burns in oxygen to produce carbon dioxide and water. If 7.9 g of acetylene burns in excess oxygen and produces 5.0 g of water, what it the percent yield for the reaction? (*Answer: 91%*)

2. Nitrogen and hydrogen react to form ammonia. If 25.0 g of nitrogen reacts with excess hydrogen to form 16.5 g of NH_3, what is the percent yield of the reaction? (*Answer: 54.3%*)

Math Refresher: Sample and Practice Problems

Rate Laws

The chemical equation and the rate law for the reaction between nitrogen oxide and ozone are shown. What will be the effect on the reaction rate if the concentration of O_3 is raised from 2.00 M to 4.00 M?

$$NO\ (g) + O_3\ (g) \rightarrow NO_2\ (g) + O_2\ (g)$$

$$rate = k[NO][O_3]$$

Analyze   Although the exact rate has not been given, the rate law indicates the relationship of each component to the reaction rate. You need to use this rate law to determine the effect on the rate each change will have.

Plan   The rate law shows that the concentrations of nitrogen oxide and ozone are directly related to the rate of reaction. You can use this information to solve the problem.

Solve   Initially, the concentration of O_3 is 2.00 M. Its value according to the rate law is

$$[O_3] = [2.00] = 2.00$$

If the $[O_3]$ is increased from 2.00 M to 4.00 M, the concentration is doubled.

Therefore, if the concentration of O_3 is doubled, the rate will increase by a factor of two.

Evaluate   The answer shows that the rate law is directly proportional to changes in the concentration of O_3.

PRACTICE PROBLEMS

1. The chemical equation and the rate law for the reaction between nitrogen dioxide and oxygen are

    $$N_2O_2\ (g) + O_2\ (g) \rightarrow 2NO_2\ (g)$$

    $$rate = k[N_2O_2][O_2]$$

    What will be the effect on the reaction rate if the concentration of O_2 is lowered from 2.50 M to 1.25 M? (*Answer: The rate is reduced by half.*)

2. The chemical equation and the rate law for the reaction of nitrogen oxide with itself are

    $$2\ NO\ (g) \rightarrow N_2O_2\ (g)$$

    $$rate = k[NO]^2$$

    What will be the effect on the reaction rate if the concentration of NO is tripled? (*Answer: The reaction rate increases by a factor of 8.*)

Math Refresher: Sample and Practice Problems

Solubility Products

At 25°C, the concentration of Mn^{2+} ions in a saturated solution of $MnCO_3$ is 4.73×10^{-6} M. What is the value of the K_{sp} for $MnCO_3$?

Analyze   You are asked to find the value of the solubility product for an ionic compound.

Plan   You must first write the equation for the solubility equilibrium and the solubility product expression. Then you can insert the concentration of ions into the expression to find the value of the K_{sp}.

Solve   The solubility equilibrium equation is

$$2MnCO_3 \rightleftharpoons Mn^{2+} (aq) + CO_3^{2-} (aq)$$

The solubility product expression is

$$K_{sp} = [Mn^{2+}] [CO_3^{2-}]$$

You know $[Mn^{2+}]$. You also know from the equation that 1 CO_3^{2-} ion is produced for every Mn^{2+} ion. So $[CO_3^{2-}]$ is equal to $[Mn^{2+}]$. Thus,

$$[Mn^{2+}] = [CO_3^{2-}] = 4.73 \times 10^{-6} \text{ M}$$

$$K_{sp} = (4.73 \times 10^{-6} \text{ M}) (4.73 \times 10^{-6} \text{ M})$$

$$K_{sp} = 2.23 \times 10^{-11}$$

Evaluate   Because at equilibrium the concentration of Mn^{2+} ions is small, you would expect K_{sp} to be small, and it is.

PRACTICE PROBLEMS

1. At 25°C, the concentration of F^{2-} ions in a saturated solution of CaF_2 is 2.1×10^{-4} M. What is the value of the K_{sp} for CaF_2? *(Answer: 3.9×10^{-11})*

2. At 25°C, the concentration of Ag^+ ions in a saturated solution of AgI is 4.2×10^{-15} M. What is the value of the K_{sp} for AgI? *(Answer: 8.3×10^{-17})*

Math Refresher: Sample and Practice Problems

Standard Enthalpy Change

How much heat will be released if 2.50 mol of NaOH (s) is dissolved in water? Assume that $\Delta H° = -445$ kJ.

Analyze   You are asked to calculate the amount of heat released when 2.50 mol of sodium hydroxide is dissolved in water. You are given the $\Delta H°$.

Plan   The given $\Delta H°$ corresponds to 1 mol of NaOH dissolving in water. This gives you the conversion factor relating moles of NaOH to the amount of heat released.

Solve   Multiply the number of moles of NaOH by the $\Delta H°$.

$$2.50 \; \cancel{\text{mol NaOH}} \; (s) \times \frac{-445 \text{ kJ}}{1 \; \cancel{\text{mol NaOH}}} = -1110 \text{ kJ}$$

Evaluate   The minus sign tells you that heat was released when the NaOH dissolved in water. The quantity of heat released, 1110 kJ, is much greater than the $\Delta H°$. This makes sense because there are more moles of NaOH.

PRACTICE PROBLEMS

1. The combustion of sulfur in excess oxygen produces sulfur trioxide, SO_3.

$$2 \text{ S } (s) + 3 \text{ O2 } (g) \rightarrow 2 \text{ SO}_3 \text{ } (g)$$

$$\Delta H° = -790 \text{ kJ}$$

   How much heat is released if 3.20 mol of sulfur is burned? *(Answer: −2530 kJ)*

2. The combustion of carbon in excess oxygen produces carbon dioxide, CO_2.

$$C \text{ } (s) + O_2 \text{ } (g) \rightarrow CO_2 \text{ } (g)$$

$$\Delta H° = -394 \text{ kJ}$$

   How much heat is released if 5.00 mol of carbon is burned? *(Answer: −1970 kJ)*

Math Refresher: Sample and Practice Problems

Stoichiometry

How many moles of C_2H_2 are needed to react with 3.8 moles of oxygen? The equation for the reaction is $2\ C_2H_2 + 5\ O_2 \rightarrow 4\ CO_2 + 2\ H_2O$.

Analyze   The number of moles for one reactant is given and you are asked to calculate the number of moles of the other reactant.

Plan   You must first determine the molar ratio between the two reactants and then use this ratio to solve the problem.

Solve   The molar ratio of O_2 to C_2H_2 is 5:2. There are 3.8 moles O_2. Therefore,

$$3.8\ \cancel{mol\ O_2} \times \frac{5\ mol\ C_2H_2}{2\ \cancel{mol\ O_2}} = 9.5\ mol\ C_2H_2$$

So, 9.5 moles of C_2H_2 are needed to react completely with 3.8 moles of O_2.

Evaluate   Because the molar ratio is of O_2 to C_2H_2 is 5:2, two and a half times the number of moles of C_2H_2 react with O_2. The answer should be two and a half times as much as the amount of O_2, which it is.

PRACTICE PROBLEMS

1. How many moles of $AgNO_3$ are needed to react with 18.74 moles of Cu? The equation for the reaction is $2\ AgNO_3 + Cu \rightarrow Cu(NO_3)_2 + 2\ Ag$. (*Answer: 9.37 moles of Cu*)

2. How many moles of O_2 are needed to react with 15.5 moles of C_4H_{10}? The equation for the reaction is $2\ C_4H_{10} + 13\ O_2 \rightarrow 8\ CO_2 + 10\ H_2O$. (*Answer: 101 moles of O_2*)

Math Refresher: Sample and Practice Problems

Titration Calculation

In a titration, 28.5 mL of 1.1 M NaOH neutralized 39.0 mL of an acetic acid solution. What is the concentration of acetic acid?

Analyze   At the equivalence point of a titration, the 28.5 mL of 1.1 M NaOH has completely neutralized the 39 mL of acetic acid.

Plan   To solve each of these problems, use the following equation.

$$\text{total moles } H^+ = \text{total moles } OH^-$$
$$\text{(at the end point)}$$

Solve   For both OH^- and H^+, the total number of moles equals the concentration times the volume. The concentration of H^+ is unknown.

$$\text{total moles } OH^- = 28.5 \text{ mL} \times 1.1 \text{ mol/L}$$
$$\text{total moles } H^+ = 39.0 \text{ mL} \times [H^+]$$

Now set these expressions equal to each other and solve for $[H^+]$:

$$\text{total moles } H^+ = \text{total moles } OH^-$$
$$39.0 \text{ mL} \times [H^+] = 28.5 \text{ mL} \times 1.1 \text{ mol/L}$$
$$[H^+] = \frac{(28.5 \text{ mL} \times 1.1 \text{ mol/L})}{39.0 \text{ mL}}$$
$$[H^+] = 0.80 \text{ mol/L}$$

Because acetic acid yields one H^+ ion per molecule, the concentration of acetic acid is also 0.80 mole per liter, or 0.80 M.

Evaluate   28.5 mL of NaOH solution neutralized a larger volume (39.0 mL) of acetic acid solution. Therefore, it makes sense that the acetic acid solution is less concentrated than the NaOH solution.

PRACTICE PROBLEMS

1. In a titration, 23.2 mL of 0.750 M HCl neutralized 41.4 mL of an NH_4OH solution. What is the concentration of ammonium hydroxide? (*Answer: 0.420 M*)

2. In a titration, 17.7 mL of 0.256 M NaOH neutralized 5.6 mL of a sulfuric acid solution. What is the concentration of sulfuric acid? (*Answer: 0.405 M*)

Periodic Table

1 1A								

Key

6
C
Carbon
12.011
$[He]2s^22p^2$

— Atomic number
— Element symbol
— Element name
— Atomic mass
— Electron configuration

1	1 **H** Hydrogen 1.00794 $1s^1$	2 2A								
2	3 **Li** Lithium 6.941 $[He]2s^1$	4 **Be** Beryllium 9.01218 $[He]2s^2$								
3	11 **Na** Sodium 22.98977 $[Ne]3s^1$	12 **Mg** Magnesium 24.305 $[Ne]3s^2$	3 3B	4 4B	5 5B	6 6B	7 7B	8	9 8B
4	19 **K** Potassium 39.0983 $[Ar]4s^1$	20 **Ca** Calcium 40.078 $[Ar]4s^2$	21 **Sc** Scandium 44.9559 $[Ar]4s^23d^1$	22 **Ti** Titanium 47.88 $[Ar]4s^23d^2$	23 **V** Vanadium 50.9415 $[Ar]4s^23d^3$	24 **Cr** Chromium 51.996 $[Ar]4s^13d^5$	25 **Mn** Manganese 54.9380 $[Ar]4s^23d^5$	26 **Fe** Iron 55.847 $[Ar]4s^23d^6$	27 **Co** Cobalt 58.9332 $[Ar]4s^23d^7$
5	37 **Rb** Rubidium 85.4678 $[Kr]5s^1$	38 **Sr** Strontium 87.62 $[Kr]5s^2$	39 **Y** Yttrium 88.9059 $[Kr]5s^24d^1$	40 **Zr** Zirconium 91.224 $[Kr]5s^24d^2$	41 **Nb** Niobium 92.9064 $[Kr]5s^14d^4$	42 **Mo** Molybdenum 95.94 $[Kr]5s^14d^5$	43 **Tc** Technetium (98) $[Kr]5s^24d^5$	44 **Ru** Ruthenium 101.07 $[Kr]5s^14d^7$	45 **Rh** Rhodium 102.9055 $[Kr]5s^14d^8$
6	55 **Cs** Cesium 132.9054 $[Xe]6s^1$	56 **Ba** Barium 137.33 $[Xe]6s^2$	71 **Lu** Lutetium 174.967 $[Xe]6s^24f^{14}5d^1$	72 **Hf** Hafnium 178.49 $[Xe]6s^24f^{14}5d^2$	73 **Ta** Tantalum 180.9479 $[Xe]6s^24f^{14}5d^3$	74 **W** Tungsten 183.85 $[Xe]6s^24f^{14}5d^4$	75 **Re** Rhenium 186.207 $[Xe]6s^24f^{14}5d^5$	76 **Os** Osmium 190.2 $[Xe]6s^24f^{14}5d^6$	77 **Ir** Iridium 192.22 $[Xe]6s^24f^{14}5d^7$
7	87 **Fr** Francium (223) $[Rn]7s^1$	88 **Ra** Radium 226.0254 $[Rn]7s^2$	103 **Lr** Lawrencium (260) $[Rn]7s^25f^{14}6d^1$	104 **Unq** Unnilquadium (261) $[Rn]7s^25f^{14}6d^2$	105 **Unp** Unnilpentium (262) $[Rn]7s^25f^{14}6d^3$	106 **Sg*** Seaborgium (263) $[Rn]7s^25f^{14}6d^4$	107 **Uns** Unnilseptium (262) $[Rn]7s^25f^{14}6d^5$	108 **Uno** Unniloctium (265) $[Rn]7s^25f^{14}6d^6$	109 **Une** Unnilennium (266) $[Rn]7s^25f^{14}6d^7$

* The name of the Element 106 has not yet been certified.

57 **La** Lanthanum 138.9055 $[Xe]6s^25d^1$	58 **Ce** Cerium 140.12 $[Xe]6s^24f^15d^1$	59 **Pr** Praseodymium 140.9077 $[Xe]6s^24f^3$	60 **Nd** Neodymium 144.24 $[Xe]6s^24f^4$	61 **Pm** Promethium (145) $[Xe]6s^24f^5$	62 **Sm** Samarium 150.36 $[Xe]6s^24f^6$
89 **Ac** Actinium 227.0278 $[Rn]7s^26d^1$	90 **Th** Thorium 232.0381 $[Rn]7s^26d^2$	91 **Pa** Protactinium 231.0359 $[Rn]7s^25f^26d^1$	92 **U** Uranium 238.0289 $[Rn]7s^25f^36d^1$	93 **Np** Neptunium 237.048 $[Rn]7s^25f^46d^1$	94 **Pu** Plutonium (244) $[Rn]7s^25f^6$

Periodic Table

						18 8A
						2 **He** Helium 4.00260 $1s^2$

			13 3A	14 4A	15 5A	16 6A	17 7A	
			5 **B** Boron 10.81 [He]$2s^22p^1$	6 **C** Carbon 12.011 [He]$2s^22p^2$	7 **N** Nitrogen 14.0067 [He]$2s^22p^3$	8 **O** Oxygen 15.9994 [He]$2s^22p^4$	9 **F** Fluorine 18.998403 [He]$2s^22p^5$	10 **Ne** Neon 20.1797 [He]$2s^22p^6$

10	11 1B	12 2B	13 **Al** Aluminum 26.98154 [Ne]$3s^23p^1$	14 **Si** Silicon 28.0855 [Ne]$3s^23p^2$	15 **P** Phosphorus 30.97376 [Ne]$3s^23p^3$	16 **S** Sulfur 32.066 [Ne]$3s^23p^4$	17 **Cl** Chlorine 35.453 [Ne]$3s^23p^5$	18 **Ar** Argon 39.948 [Ne]$3s^23p^6$
28 **Ni** Nickel 58.69 [Ar]$4s^23d^8$	29 **Cu** Copper 63.546 [Ar]$4s^13d^{10}$	30 **Zn** Zinc 65.39 [Ar]$4s^23d^{10}$	31 **Ga** Gallium 69.72 [Ar]$4s^23d^{10}4p^1$	32 **Ge** Germanium 72.61 [Ar]$4s^23d^{10}4p^2$	33 **As** Arsenic 74.9216 [Ar]$4s^23d^{10}4p^3$	34 **Se** Selenium 78.96 [Ar]$4s^23d^{10}4p^4$	35 **Br** Bromine 79.904 [Ar]$4s^23d^{10}4p^5$	36 **Kr** Krypton 83.80 [Ar]$4s^23d^{10}4p^6$
46 **Pd** Palladium 106.42 [Kr]$4d^{10}$	47 **Ag** Silver 107.8682 [Kr]$5s^14d^{10}$	48 **Cd** Cadmium 112.41 [Kr]$5s^24d^{10}$	49 **In** Indium 114.82 [Kr]$5s^24d^{10}5p^1$	50 **Sn** Tin 118.710 [Kr]$5s^24d^{10}5p^2$	51 **Sb** Antimony 121.757 [Kr]$5s^24d^{10}5p^3$	52 **Te** Tellurium 127.60 [Kr]$5s^24d^{10}5p^4$	53 **I** Iodine 126.9045 [Kr]$5s^24d^{10}5p^5$	54 **Xe** Xenon 131.29 [Kr]$5s^24d^{10}5p^6$
78 **Pt** Platinum 195.08 [Xe]$6s^14f^{14}5d^9$	79 **Au** Gold 196.9665 [Xe]$6s^14f^{14}5d^{10}$	80 **Hg** Mercury 200.59 [Xe]$6s^24f^{14}5d^{10}$	81 **Tl** Thallium 204.383 [Xe]$6s^24f^{14}5d^{10}6p^1$	82 **Pb** Lead 207.2 [Xe]$6s^24f^{14}5d^{10}6p^2$	83 **Bi** Bismuth 208.9804 [Xe]$6s^24f^{14}5d^{10}6p^3$	84 **Po** Polonium (209) [Xe]$6s^24f^{14}5d^{10}6p^4$	85 **At** Astatine (210) [Xe]$6s^24f^{14}5d^{10}6p^5$	86 **Rn** Radon (222) [Xe]$6s^24f^{14}5d^{10}6p^6$
110 **Uun** Ununnilium (269) [Rn]$7s^25f^{14}6d^8$	111 **Uuu** Unununium (272) [Rn]$7s^25f^{14}6d^9$	112 **Uub** Ununbium (277) [Rn]$7s^25f^{14}6d^{10}$						

63 **Eu** Europium 151.96 [Xe]$6s^24f^7$	64 **Gd** Gadolinium 157.25 [Xe]$6s^24f^75d^1$	65 **Tb** Terbium 158.9254 [Xe]$6s^24f^9$	66 **Dy** Dysprosium 162.50 [Xe]$6s^24f^{10}$	67 **Ho** Holmium 164.9304 [Xe]$6s^24f^{11}$	68 **Er** Erbium 167.26 [Xe]$6s^24f^{12}$	69 **Tm** Thulium 168.9342 [Xe]$6s^24f^{13}$	70 **Yb** Ytterbium 173.04 [Xe]$6s^24f^{14}$
95 **Am** Americium (243) [Rn]$7s^25f^7$	96 **Cm** Curium (247) [Rn]$7s^25f^76d^1$	97 **Bk** Berkelium (247) [Rn]$7s^25f^9$	98 **Cf** Californium (251) [Rn]$7s^25f^{10}$	99 **Es** Einsteinium (252) [Rn]$7s^25f^{11}$	100 **Fm** Fermium (257) [Rn]$7s^25f^{12}$	101 **Md** Mendelevium (258) [Rn]$7s^25f^{13}$	102 **No** Nobelium (259) [Rn]$7s^25f^{14}$

Glossary

absolute zero: point at which particles of matter have no kinetic energy and therefore stop moving

acid dissociation constant (K_a): constant that indicates the strength of an acid; derived from the equilibrium constant for the acid's dissociation in water

acid: compound that donates a proton or hydronium (H_3O^+) ion

acidic hydrogen: hydrogen atom that an acid may lose as an ion of H_3O^+

activated complex: short-lived structure that has properties of both the reactants and products

activity series: list of elements organized according to the ease with which they undergo certain chemical reactions

actual yield: amount of product obtained from a chemical reaction

alcohol: hydrocarbon in which one or more hydrogen atoms has been replaced by a hydroxyl group (R—OH)

aldehyde: hydrocarbon derivative with a carbonyl group on the end of a hydrocarbon chain

alkali metal: element in the Group 1A of the periodic table

alkaline earth metal: element in the Group 2A of the periodic table

alkane: hydrocarbon containing only single bonds

alkene: hydrocarbon containing at least one double bond

alkyne: hydrocarbon containing at least one triple bond

allotrope: form of an element that has a bonding pattern different from other forms of the same element

alloy: solid solution in which the atoms of two or more metals are uniformly mixed

amines: hydrocarbon derivative in which an amino group is attached to a hydrocarbon chain (R—NH_2)

amino acid: hydrocarbon derivative containing an amino group and a carboxyl group

amorphous solid: solid in which the arrangement of the particles lack a regular, repeating pattern

amphoteric: description of any substance that can react as either an acid or a base

amplitude: wave height measured from the origin to its crest or peak

anhydrous: substance that is without water

anion: negative ion

anode: electrode at which oxidation occurs; has a negative charge

aqueous: solution in which water is the solvent

atmospheric pressure: pressure exerted by the weight of air in the atmosphere

atom: smallest particle of an element that retains the chemical identity of the element

atomic mass unit (amu): unit by which the mass of an atom or atomic particle is expressed; unit of mass equal to 1/12 the mass of a carbon-12 atom

atomic mass: weighted average of the masses of the existing isotopes of an element

atomic number: number of protons in the nucleus of an atom

atomic radius: distance between the center of the nucleus of an atom and the outermost electrons

atomic theory of matter: theory proposed by Thomas Dalton stating that elements are composed of atoms, all atoms of a given element are identical but different from atoms of other elements, atoms are neither created nor destroyed in a chemical reaction, and a given compound always has the same relative numbers and kinds of atoms.

Avogadro's Law: equal volumes of gases at the same temperature and pressure contain an equal number of particles

ball-and-stick model: three-dimensional physical model of molecular shape in which a ball represents atoms and sticks represent bonds

barometer: instrument used to measure atmospheric pressure

base: compound that accepts a proton, or H_3O^+ ion

base dissociation constant (K_b): constant that indicates the strength of a base; derived from the equilibrium constant (K_{eq}) for the base's dissociation in water

benzene: ring-shaped hydrocarbon that has hybrid of single and double bonds

binary acid: acid consisting of hydrogen and one other element

binary ionic compound: ionic compound consisting of two elements

bond angle: geometric angle between two adjacent bonds in a molecule

boiling point elevation: colligative property in which the boiling point of a solvent is raised when a solute is dissolved

Boyle's Law: the pressure and volume of a sample of gas at constant temperature are inversely proportional to each other

branched alkane: alkane molecule with at least one carbon atom bonded to more than two other carbon atoms

buffer: solution in which adding small amounts of acid or base does not markedly change the pH

buffer capacity: amount of acid or base that a buffer can neutralize

calorie: amount of heat needed to raise the temperature of 1 g of water by 1°C

carbohydrate: compound made from aldehydes and ketones, containing many hydroxyl groups; starches and sugars

carbonyl group: oxygen atom double-bonded to a carbon atom (C=O)

carboxyl group: combination of a carbonyl group and a hydroxyl group (—COOH)

carboxylic acid: hydrocarbon derivative containing a carboxyl group (R—COOH)

catalyst: substance that increases the rate of a reaction without itself being used up in the reaction

cathode: electrode at which reduction occurs; has a positive charge

cation: positive ion

cell potential: ability of a reaction in a voltaic cell to move electrons through a wire from one electrode to another; also called electrical potential

Charles's Law: at a constant pressure, the volume of a fixed amount of gas is directly proportional to its absolute temperature

chemical equation: condensed statement that uses chemical formulas and identifiers the reactants and products in a chemical reaction

chemical equilibrium: dynamic state in which the concentration of reactants and products involved in a reversible reaction remain constant with time because the rates of the forward and reverse reaction are equal

chemical property: characteristic of a substance that cannot be observed without altering the identity of the substance

chemical reaction: process in which one or more substances are converted into new substances with different physical and chemical properties

coefficient: whole number that precedes a reactant or product symbol or formula in a chemical equation and indicates the relative number of representative particles involved in the reaction

colligative property: property of a solution that depends upon the concentration of the solute, but not its identity

collision theory: theory explaining chemical reactions based upon the collisions of particles and the orientation and energy with which they collide

common-ion effect: shift in solubility equilibrium that occurs when the concentration of an ion that is part of the equilibrium is changed

compound: substance that contains two or more elements chemically combined in a fixed proportion

concentration: amount of solute dissolved in a given amount of solvent

condensation: change of state from a gas to a liquid

condensed states: liquid and solid states of matter; states in which a substance has a substantially higher density than in the gaseous state

conformation: structure of an organic molecule that differs from another structure by one or more bond rotations

conjugate acid: acid formed when a base gains a proton

conjugate base: base formed when an acid loses a proton

covalent bonding: chemical bond resulting from the sharing of electrons between two bonding atoms

covalent-network solid: solid in which strong covalent bonds form a network extending throughout the solid

crystalline solid: solid in which the representative particles are in a highly ordered, repeating pattern called a crystal

Dalton's Law of Partial Pressures: the sum of the partial pressures of all the components in a gas mixture is equal to the total pressure of the gas mixture

decomposition reaction: chemical reaction in which a single complex compound is broken down into two or more products

dehydration synthesis: process by which two molecules are joined and a molecule of water is removed

deposition: conversion of a gas directly into a solid without first becoming a liquid

diffusion: movement of one substance through another

dilute solution: solution with a low concentration of solvent

dipole: molecule in which the centers of positive and negative charge are not the same

direct combination reaction: chemical reaction in which two or more simple reactants join to form a single, more complex product

dissolution: process in which an ionic solid dissolves in a polar liquid

dosimeter: device for measuring total exposure to radiation

double covalent bond: chemical bond resulting from the sharing of two electron pairs between two atoms

double-replacement reaction: chemical reaction in which atoms or ions from two different compounds replace each other

effective collision: collision between particles that leads to the formation of products

effusion: movement of atoms or molecules through an opening so tiny that they pass through one particle at a time into an evacuated chamber

elastic: ability of a substance or object to readily spring back to its original size or shape after being squeezed, hit, or subjected to a similar disturbance

electrode: substance through which electrons enter or exit electrochemical cells; made of metal and provides a surface on which oxidation and reduction occur

electrolysis: process by which an outside source of electricity is used to drive a nonspontaneous redux reaction

electrolyte: substance that dissolves in water to form a solution that conducts electric current

electromagnetic radiation: form of energy consisting of waves made up of oscillating electric and magnetic fields at right angles to each other

electron affinity: energy change that occurs when an atom gains an electron

electron configuration: distribution of electrons among the orbitals of an atom

electron: negatively charged particle within an atom

electronegativity: property of an element that indicates how strongly an atom of that element attracts electrons in a chemical bond

electroplating: process in which electrolysys is used to deposit a thin coating of a protective metal on an object

element: substance that cannot be separated into simpler substances by a chemical change

elementary step: individual reaction in an overall reaction mechanism

empirical formula: chemical formula that gives the simplest whole-number ratio of atoms of elements in a compound

end point: point in a titration at which an indicator changes color to show that equivalent quantities of acid and base have reacted

endothermic: absorbing heat

energy: capacity to do work or transfer heat

enthalpy: heat content of a system at constant pressure

entropy: quantitative measure of disorder or randomness of a system

equilibrium vapor pressure: pressure exerted by a vapor in equilibrium with its liquid

equivalence point: point at which there are equal quantities of hydronium ions and hydroxide ions

Glossary *(continued)*

ester: hydrocarbon in which an oxygen atom is between two carbon atoms in a hydrocarbon chain (R—O—R')

ether: derivative in which two hydrocarbon chains are attached to the same oxygen atom (R—O—R')

evaporation: process by which molecules of a liquid escape from the surface of the liquid and enter the gaseous, or vapor state

exothermic: releasing heat

expected yield: amount of a product that should be produced by a chemical reaction according to stoichiometric calculations

family: vertical column of the periodic table that contains elements with similar electron configuration; also known as a group

formula mass: sum of the atomic masses of all atoms in a compound as represented in a chemical

freezing point: temperature at which the solid and liquid form of a substance exist in equilibrium

frequency: number of waves that pass a certain point in a given amount of time

functional group: atom or group of atoms that gives a molecule a characteristic chemical behavior

gas: state in which matter has no definite shape or volume

Geiger counter: device used to measure radioactivity

Gibbs free energy: energy equal to the energy change for a reaction minus the product of its entropy change times the absolute temperature

groups: vertical column of the periodic table that contains elements with similar electron configuration; also known as a family

half-cell: container in which a half reaction of a redox reaction occurs

half-life: time it takes for one half of a sample of a radioisotope to decay

halocarbon: hydrocarbon in which one or more hydrogen atoms has been replaced by a halogen

halogen: reactive, nonmetallic element in Group 7A of the periodic table

heat of fusion: heat necessary to convert a given amount of a solid into a liquid

heat of vaporization: amount of heat necessary to vaporize a given amount of liquid

heating curve: plot of the temperature of a sample as a function of time

heterogeneous mixture: mixture in which the particles are not uniformly intermingled and that therefore has visibly different parts

hexose: monosaccharide, or simple sugar, that has six carbon atoms

homogeneous mixture: mixture made up of uniformly intermingled particles that therefore does not contain visibly different parts

hydrate: substance combined chemically with water in a definite ratio

hybrid orbital: orbital of electrons that has a combination of shapes and properties of other atomic orbitals

hydration: process by which water molecules pull solute particles into solution and form a sphere around them

hydrocarbon: compound consisting of carbon and hydrogen atoms

hydrogenation: addition of hydrogen to a double or triple bond

hydrolysis: reaction in which water is added to break a reactant into two molecules

hydronium ion (H_3O^+): ion formed by the addition of a proton to a water molecule

hydroxyl group: combination of an oxygen atom and a hydrogen atom (—OH)

ideal gas: theoretical gas described perfectly by the kinetic-molecular theory

immiscible: inability of a liquid to form a solution with another liquid in all proportions

indicators: substance that changes color at certain pH values and can therefore be used to roughly determine whether a sample is an acid or a base

insoluble: inability of a substance to dissolve in another substance

intermediate product: substance produced in one step of a reaction mechanism and consumed in a later step

intermolecular force: relatively weak force of attraction that exists between neighboring molecules

intramolecular force: force of attraction that exists within a molecule to hold it together

ion: atom or group of atoms that has a positive or negative charge because it lost or gained electrons

ion product: calculation determined by inserting concentration at a given point in a reaction into the solubility product expression; value can be compared with the solubility product to determine whether a solution form a precipitate

ionic bond: chemical bond resulting from the transfer of electrons from one bonding atom to another

ionic compound: compound of positive and negative ions combined so that the charges are neutralized; formed from a metal and a nonmetal

ionization energy: energy required to remove the most loosely held electron from an atom

ion-product constant (K_w): for water, equal to $[H_3O^+][OH^-] = 1.0 \times 10^{-14}$ at 25°C

isotope: atom that has the same number of protons as another atom, but that has a different number of neutrons

joule (J): basic unit of energy in the International System of Units

ketone: hydrocarbon derivative that has a carbonyl group within a hydrocarbon chain

kinetic energy: energy of motion

kinetic-molecular theory: model that explains the physical properties of gases based on the submicroscopic behavior of gas particles; in mathematical form, it yields the ideal gas equation

law of conservation of energy: natural law describing the fact that energy is not created nor destroyed in any process

law of conservation of matter: natural law describing the fact that matter is neither created nor destroyed in any process

law of constant composition: natural law describing the fact that a given compound always contains the same elements in the same proportions

Le Chatelier's principle: principle that states that a reversible reaction at equilibrium will shift to offset a stress, or change in conditions, imposed on a system

limiting reactant: reactant that is completely used up in a chemical reaction and that therefore determines the maximum amount of product that can be formed

lipid: water-insoluble molecule with oily or waxy properties

liquid: state in which matter does not hold a definite shape but occupies a definite volume

manometer: instrument used to measure the pressure of a gas in a closed container

mass number: sum of the number of protons and neutrons in the nucleus of a given atom

mass–mass problems: stoichiometric problem in which the mass of one substance is determined from the mass of another substance in the reaction; solved by using the molar ratio indicated in the balanced chemical equation

mass–volume problems: stoichiometric problem in which the volume of one substance is determined from the mass of another substance in the reaction; solved by using the molar ratio of the two substances as indicated in the balanced chemical equation

matter: anything that has mass and volume

matter wave: term used to describe the wavelike behavior of particles

metal: element that typically has a high melting point, is ductile, malleable, shiny, and a good conductor of electricity; found on the left side of the periodic table

metallic bonds: bonds that hold metals together; formed by achieving a stable electron arrangement by sharing their valance electrons

miscible: ability of a liquid to form a solution with another liquid in all proportions

molality (m): concentration of a solution determined by the number of moles of solute per kilogram of solvent

molar mass: mass in grams of 1 mole of a substance

molar volume: volume of 1 mole of an ideal gas at standard conditions (1 atm, 0°C); equal to 22.4 L

molarity (M): concentration of a solution determined by the number of moles of solute per liter of solution

mole fraction: concentration of a solution determined by the number of moles of one substance is determined from the number of moles of another substance in the reaction; solved by using the molar ratio indicated by the balanced chemical equation

mole: quantity of a substance that has a mass in grams numerically equal to its formula mass; equal to 6.02×10^{23} representative particles

molecular formula: chemical formula that indicates the number of each atom in a molecular compound

molecular substance: substance that has atoms held together by covalent bonds

molecule: neutral group of atoms united by covalent bonds

mole-mole problem: stoichiometric problem in which the number of moles of one substance is determined from the number of moles of another substance in the reaction; solved by using the molar ratio indicated by the balanced chemical equation

monatomic: ion formed from a single atom

monomer: small molecule that joins with other simliar molecules to make a polymer

monosaccharide: simple sugar; monomer of a carbohydrate

neutralization reaction: reaction in which an acid and a base react to form a salt and water

neutrons: neutral particle within the nucleus of an atom

noble gas: inactive element in Group 8A of the periodic table

nonelectrolyte: a substance that dissolves in water to form a solution that does not conduct electric current

nonmetal: element that has a low melting point and a dull surface, breaks easily, is a poor conductor of heat and electricity, and tends to gain electrons in chemical reactions

nonpolar: description of a bond that has an even distribution of charge due to an equal sharing of bonding electrons

nuclear bombardment reaction: reaction in which a high-speed particle collides with a nucleus to produce a different nucleus

nuclear chain reaction: series of fission reactions in which products of one reaction initiate further reactions

nuclear fission: splitting of an atomic nucleus

nuclear fusion: joining of two atomic nuclei

nuclear reaction: process that changes the composition of a nucleus

nucleic acid: polymer made up of nucleotides

nucleotide: monomer of a nucleic acid made up of a 5-carbon sugar, a phosphate group, and a nitrogen base

nucleus: concentrated core of an atom, which contains protons and neutrons

organic chemistry: study of carbon compounds

osmosis: flow of water molecules from a dilute solution to a concentrated solution across a semipermeable membrane

osmotic pressure: pressure required to prevent osmosis

oxidation: reaction in which the atoms or ions of an element lose one or more electrons and thus attain a more positive oxidation state (higher oxidation number)

oxidation number: number assigned to the atoms in a molecule that shows the general distribution of electrons among bonded atoms; equal to the charge in ionic compounds and the charge assigned to atoms according to electronegativity rules for covalent compounds; algebraic sum of oxidation numbers in a molecule is zero

oxidation-reduction reactions: chemical process in which elements undergo a change in oxidation number; redox reaction

oxidizing agent: substance that gains electrons or attains a more negative oxidation state (lower oxidation number) during an oxidation-reduction reaction

oxy acid: acid that contains hydrogen, oxygen, and one other element

pentose: monosaccharide, or simple sugar, that has five carbon atoms

peptide bond: covalent bond joining two amino acids

percent yield: actual yield divided by the expected yield times 100 percent

Glossary (continued)

period: horizontal row of elements in the periodic table

periodic law: natural law that states that the physical and chemical properties of the elements are periodic functions of their atomic numbers

periodic table: arrangement of the elements in order of their atomic numbers so that elements with similar electron configurations are located in the same column

phase diagram: plot of the state of a sample as a function of temperature and pressure

phospholipid: lipid made up of an alcohol, fatty acids, and a phosphate group

photon: quantum of electromagnetic energy

physical property: characteristic of a substance that can be observed without altering the identity of the substance

plasma: state of matter at extremely high temperature in which atoms are highly ionized

polar: description of a bond that has an uneven distribution of charge due to an unequal sharing of electrons

polyatomic: charged group of covalently bonded atoms

polymer: large molecule consisting of small repeating units called monomers

polysaccharide: polymer formed when three or more monosaccharides join together; complex sugar

potential energy: energy possessed by an object because of its position or arrangement of its particles

principal energy level: one of a limited number of energy levels in an atom

product: substance formed during a chemical reaction

protein: large amino acid polymer

proton: positively charged particle within the nucleus of an atom

pure substance: substance made of one kind of material with a unique set of chemical and physical properties

radiant energy: energy in the form of waves

radioisotope: radioactive isotope

rate-determining step: slowest elementary step in a reaction mechanism

rate law: equation that shows the relationship of the rate of a reaction to the concentrations of substances involved in the reaction

reactant: substance that enters into a chemical reaction

reaction mechanism: sequence of steps leading from reactants to products

reaction quotient: calculation determined by inserting the concentration of reactant and products of a reversible reaction at a given point into the equilibrium constant to determine if a reaction is at equilibrium

reaction rate: rate or speed at which a reaction takes place; change in the concentration of reactants and products per unit time

redox reaction: chemical process in which elements undergo a change in oxidation number; oxidation-reduction reaction

reducing agent: substance that loses electrons or attains a more positive oxidation state (higher oxidation number) during an oxidation-reduction reaction

reduction: reaction in which the atoms or ions of an element gain one or more electrons and thus attain a more negative oxidation state (lower oxidation number)

reversible reaction: chemical reaction in which the products can react to form the original products

salt: ionic compound formed from the anion of an acid and cation of a base

saturated: description of a solution that contains as much dissolved solute as it can under existing conditions

saturated hydrocarbon: carbon chain that is filled to capacity with hydrogen atoms

self-ionization: chemical reaction in which two molecules of the same substance, usually water, react to produce ions

semimetal: element that does not have metallic properties; found on the right side of the periodic table

single covalent bond: chemical bond resulting from the sharing of an electron pair between two atoms

single-replacement reaction: chemical reaction in which an uncombined element replaces an element that is part of a compound

solid: state in which matter holds a definite shape and volume

solubility: amount of solute that dissolves in a given amount of solvent at a given temperature to form a saturated solution

solubility equilibrium: condition that exists when the rate at which an ionic solid dissolves in a solution is equal to the rate at which ions leave the solution to regenerate the solid

solubility product: equilibrium constant for a solution of a sparingly soluble ionic compound; equal to the product of the concentrations of ions in solution, each raised to the powers indicated by their coefficients in the balanced equation

soluble: ability of a substance to dissolve in another substance

solute: substance that is dissolved in a solvent to form a solution

solution: homogeneous mixture of two or more substances in a single physical state

solvation: process in which solvent particles pull solute particles into solution and form a sphere around them

solvent: substance that does the dissolving in a solution

spontaneous chemical reaction: reaction that proceeds on its own, without outside intervention

standard solution: reactant of known concentration used in acid-base titration

steroid: lipid with a skeletal structure consisting of four carbon rings

stoichiometry: study of quantitative relationships that can be derived from chemical formulas and equations

strong nuclear force: force of attraction between the particles in the nucleus of an atom; in a stable atom, the strong nuclear force overcomes the force of repulsion between protons

structural formula: formula that indicates how the atoms in a molecule are bonded to each other

structural isomer: molecule with the same molecular formula but with different structural formulas

sublimation: conversion of a solid directly into a gas, without first becoming a liquid

supersaturated: description of a solution that contains more dissolved solute than a saturated solution

surface tension: imbalance of attractive forces at the surface of a liquid that causes the surface to behave as if it had a thin film across it

transistion state: brief period when bonds are disrupted and new bonds are formed

trigliceride: ester of glycerol and three fatty acids; term for fats and oils in general

triple covalent bonds: chemical bond resulting from the sharing of three electron pairs between two atoms

unsaturated: description of a solution that contains less dissolved solute than it can under existing conditions

valence electrons: electron in the outermost energy level of an atom

vaporization: change of state from liquid to gas

vapor point reduction: colligative property in which the pressure of the vapor over a solvent is reduced when a solute is dissolved

viscosity: resistance to motion that exists between the molecules of a liquid when they move past each other

visible spectrum: portion of the electromagnetic spectrum that can be seen with the unaided eye

voltaic cell: electrochemical cell that produces electricity by means of redox reactions

volume–volume problem: stoichiometric problem in which the volume of one substance is determined from the volume of another substance in a reaction; solved by using the molar ratio of the two substances as indicated by the balanced chemical equation

VSEPR (valence-shell electron pair repulsion) theory: theory that explains that in small molecules, valence electrons are arranged as far apart from each other as possible; can be used to predict the shape of molecules

wavelength: distance between successive crests

work: capacity to move an object over distance against a resisting force.